Trevor Dennis has long been passionate about opening the world of exciting and challenging biblical scholarship to a wider audience. For nearly twelve years, he taught Old Testament studies at Salisbury and Wells Theological College (now Sarum College), before joining the staff of Chester Cathedral as Canon Chancellor. In this role he had an education brief, and he retained this when he was given the additional responsibilities of Vice Dean. He retired in 2010, but has continued with his writing and with speaking to Christian groups of various denominations all over the country. He attends his parish church and the local Quaker Meeting on alternate Sundays. This is his fourteenth book published by SPCK. The others comprise four volumes on Old Testament narratives: *Lo and Behold* (1991), *Sarah Laughed* (1994), *Looking God in the Eye* (1998) and *Face to Face with God* (1999); two other books on the Gospels: *The Christmas Stories* (2007) and *The Easter Stories* (2008); six collections of stories and poems composed originally for preaching: *Speaking of God* (1992), *Imagining God* (1997), *The Three Faces of Christ* (1999), *Keeping God Company* (2002), *God Treads Softly Here* (2004) and *God in Our Midst* (2012); and a volume written with Ken Lewis, *The Circle of Peace: An Antidote to Distress* (2015). In addition, Lion Hudson published *The Book of Books* in 2003, his retelling of some of the finest stories and poems in the Bible for children and adults. He is married to Caroline, and they have four children and eight grandchildren.

THE GOSPEL BEYOND
THE GOSPELS

Trevor Dennis

First published in Great Britain in 2017

Society for Promoting Christian Knowledge
36 Causton Street
London SW1P 4ST
www.spck.org.uk

British Library Cataloguing-in-Publication Data
A catalogue record for this book is available from the British Library

ISBN 978–0–281–07533–1
eBook ISBN 978–0–281–07534–8

Typeset by Manila Typesetting Company
First printed in Great Britain by Ashford Colour Press
Subsequently digitally reprinted in Great Britain

eBook by Manila Typesetting Company

Produced on paper from sustainable forests

In memory of a dear friend,
Janis Lewis,
who died, too soon,
during the making of this book

Contents

Contents

Introduction

We can so easily take the Gospels for granted. It is truly astonishing, however, that four narratives of such literary brilliance and theological profundity were composed within a few decades of Jesus' death and resurrection. Yet they fail, as all Christians and their writings do, to come to terms in every respect with what Jesus taught and with how he lived and died. They point beyond themselves to a more radical gospel they sometimes obfuscate or even deny. They provide the signposts, go ahead of us on the journey, and in many ways articulate that other gospel with great power. Sometimes, however, they do not look hard enough or sufficiently maintain their gaze; sometimes they retreat to safer ground; sometimes they lead us astray.

This book will explore that theme, not by any comprehensive treatment (that would require a very big volume) but by means of a number of examples.

In our first chapter we will focus on some of those people in the Gospels who encounter Jesus and whose lives are profoundly changed by him. These are among the one-sceners, as we call them, people who appear in the narrative without introduction, have their one scene and then are gone. Usually the Gospels do not name them, and those we have chosen to explore are either left unnamed entirely or else, in one case, given a name which clearly does not belong to him. By swinging the spotlight onto them and holding it there, we will seek to arrive at a fuller picture of the impact Jesus had on them. We will be trying to do them honour. In the process we will discover that we are honouring Jesus, also.

Much of our discussion in that chapter will be concerned with Jesus' meetings with women (or perhaps a single woman). The second chapter will explore more systematically the part women played in Jesus' circle. We will be feeding largely on scraps, picking up hints where we can find them, since none of the Gospels do these women credit. Nonetheless, the things they do tell us are of the utmost significance, and we will reach at the end a startling conclusion.

While the second chapter ranges widely through all four Gospels, the third will confine itself to Luke, to the stunning Parable of the Two Brothers (we will explain why we call it that, rather than The Prodigal Son) and finally, and much more briefly, to a particular story within his Passion narrative. Serious and unresolved tensions within his Gospel will become apparent.

Such tensions, and more of them, will be the concern of our final chapter, which will be the most far-reaching. What kind of figure can we find in the Gospels, if we look for Jesus with a fresh and unclouded eye? What kind of God do we encounter there? To put it very simply, do we find a king and a warrior or a footwasher; a God who sits for our great fear on high throne or one who chooses to sit on a mat on the ground? That question has always been an urgent one, but in these days of Daesh and the excesses of fundamentalism in all faiths, including Christianity, it could hardly be of greater importance.

The Gospels are utterly fascinating documents, the more interesting the harder we look into them. They are magnificent, but they are flawed, and some of their material is toxic. We need to be as honest as we can about both their strengths and their weaknesses. We need to unearth their treasures, hold them in our hands, wonder at them, and then reinter them in our souls and in our living; we need also to recognize what is indefensible and refuse to take part in defending it. We need to stop taking the Gospels for gospel. We need to find the gospel beyond the Gospels, the greater Truth to which they all point.

1

'Do you see this woman?'

Turning the spotlight

When we were at university and before we were married, my wife and I went to a student production of *Hamlet*. It was a fine one, with a strong performance from the lead actor. Fifty years on we still remember it. But our most vivid memory is of the gravedigger in Act 5, Scene 1. 'Wait!' you say. 'There are two gravediggers in that scene, not just one.' Not in this production, there weren't. One was enough. We had seen the actor before in the Cambridge Footlights. He only had to walk on stage and the audience would collapse in laughter. Now *Hamlet* is a tragedy that does what it says on the tin. By Act 5 you are in desperate need of some light relief, and Shakespeare gives us the gravediggers to release the tension before once more he turns the screw. Our one gravedigger quickly had us all laughing, and the comedy continued once Hamlet and Horatio came on stage. But then it got serious, or was meant to. Hamlet began his great speech on the skull of Yorick, which the gravedigger had lifted from the ground and handed to him. 'Alas! poor Yorick. I knew him, Horatio . . .' It is one of the great speeches of a very great play, but we could hardly hear the words. The gravedigger was sitting with his legs dangling over the edge of the grave, while from up his sleeve he took a banana, peeled it, bit by bit, piece by piece, and slowly ate it. We all tried to smother our laughter. But we couldn't help it, and Hamlet's wonderful words were lost as our shoulders shook and our hands were clapped on our mouths.

You will not find a stage direction about a banana up the sleeve in Shakespeare's text! Having given the stage to the gravediggers at the start of the scene, come Hamlet's speech on the skull of Yorick he means all our attention to be turned towards the prince. But in this production we the audience effectively swung the spotlight round and shone it on the gravedigger and his banana, and then held it there.

In all four Gospels the spotlight is fixed on Jesus almost the whole time. He appears almost immediately in Mark, Matthew and John, and although Luke has a long first chapter before he is born and devotes the first 20 verses of chapter 3 to John the Baptist, every word of those passages is still designed to prepare us for Jesus' entrance. Once on stage, in any of the Gospels, he hardly ever leaves it. The Evangelists would wish us to keep our eyes on him at all times. But what if we choose not to? Or at least, what if we also pay particular attention

3

to the people around him? The Jesus of the Gospels' extraordinary narratives meets a large number of people. Often he is surrounded by a crowd, but the Gospels have many stories of his encounters with individuals, where he makes a dramatic and profound impact upon them. What happens if we turn our spotlight on these minor characters and hold it there?

The number of examples we take in this chapter will be very small, just three. That will enable us to explore them in depth, to look hard and keep looking.

We could not help ourselves in that theatre in Cambridge. That will not be the case here. We will have to make a conscious choice, and because the presence of Jesus in the story is always so beguiling, and because we have for so long done what the Evangelists wanted and kept our eyes fixed on him, we may find it hard to widen our vision and change our focus. But let us try. What will we see, I wonder? And equally important, what will we not see?

An outpouring of love

Let us begin with a famous story in Luke 7.36–50. The title of this chapter is taken from it. There are not so many stories which appear in all four Gospels, but this might seem to be one of them. It is a story of a woman anointing Jesus, and as such it has its parallels in Mark 14.3–9, Matthew 26.6–13 and John 12.1–8. In John, and only in John, the woman is named, as Mary of Bethany, and he lends her actions a very particular significance. There are other large discrepancies between these passages, however. In Mark and Matthew the woman anoints Jesus' head; in Luke and John she anoints his feet. Luke's version, the longest of the four, is the only one placed relatively early in the narrative of Jesus' ministry. The other Gospels tell of the woman as they reach the events leading to Jesus' crucifixion. For them the story has dark overtones. The woman's anointing, be it of his head or his feet, is done in preparation for Jesus' burial. Her actions speak of Jesus' imminent death and suggest that his burial will be a hurried one, with not enough time to anoint the body before it is laid in the tomb. Not so in Luke. His is not a dark story, though it has some shadows on its surface. His is almost pure love story. In truth the versions in the other Gospels are love stories also, but in Mark and Matthew, and in John too at first sight, the woman's love is more hidden and obscured by the gathering clouds, clouds that in Mark, Matthew and Luke will thicken to pitch black when Jesus hangs on the cross. In my Greek New Testament and my NRSV translation Luke's story is given the heading, 'A sinful woman forgiven'.[1] The Jewish Annotated New Testament entitles it, 'The Pharisee and the woman who loved much'[2] and that is much better. I would prefer to call it simply, 'An outpouring of love'.

When we turn the spotlight on the woman in Luke, what do we see and what do we hear? When Jesus arrives, as he will tell us later, she is there already. 'From the time I came in,' he will say to his host, 'she has not stopped kissing my feet' (7.45b). She is not, however, among the invited guests. A Pharisee called Simon has asked Jesus to eat with him, and the woman has found out about it. She has, it seems, been searching for Jesus, and has seized the opportunity given to her. Luke devotes just one verse to the preliminaries, and then cuts to the chase:

> And a woman in the city, who was a sinner, having learned that he was eating in the Pharisee's house, brought an alabaster jar of ointment.

She stood behind him at his feet, weeping, and began to bathe his feet with her tears and to dry them with her hair. Then she continued kissing his feet and anointing them with the ointment. Now when the Pharisee who had invited him saw it, he said to himself, 'If this man were a prophet, he would have known who and what kind of woman this is who is touching him – that she is a sinner.'   (Luke 7.37–39)

What is the woman's name? We do not hear that, either here or at any point in the story. This woman is a one-scener. She has her moment in the spotlight, and then disappears into the shadows. Like the majority of one-sceners in the Gospels she is anonymous. (Indeed, when some *are* named, beyond those such as Pilate or Caiaphas the high priest who were in the public eye, we find ourselves asking why they should be singled out for such honour.) We will know what to call the woman who anoints Jesus in John, but not here. That is very sad, the more so when we have the name of the Pharisee. The one who loves Jesus so remains nameless. The one who is suspicious of him, according to Luke, who has invited him, so it seems, to test him out, who is so quickly dismissive of him, who has already insulted him in not offering him the usual courtesies (as soon in the story we will learn), the one who fails to see what is going on and remains blind in his tight little world (as Luke paints him[3]), he is afforded the dignity of his name. It is not as it should be.

Yet Luke tells us a good deal about this woman, much more than hearers of her story are sometimes prepared to acknowledge. Too many notice only one word: 'sinner'. 'Prostitute,' they mutter. And then, perhaps, 'Mary of Magdala'.

New Testament scholars have long exposed that last piece of nonsense. As we have explained, John names the woman Mary. In his Gospel it is not the first time we have met her; she is introduced to us in chapter 11. On both occasions John tells us plainly that this Mary lives in Bethany near Jerusalem, with her sister Martha and her brother Lazarus. Bethany is nowhere near Magdala in Galilee. But that did not stop Pope Gregory the Great, in a sermon preached in 594, telling his congregation,

She whom Luke calls the sinful woman, whom John calls Mary, we believe to be the Mary from whom seven demons were ejected according to Mark. [Gregory is there referring to Mark 16.9, a verse about Mary of Magdala added to Mark's Gospel in the second century

and borrowed from Luke 8.2.] And what did these seven demons
signify if not all the vices? . . . It is clear, brothers, that this woman
previously used the unguent to perfume her flesh in forbidden acts.

(Gregory the Great, Homily 33)

Gregory's reading of the Gospels is sloppy, and his imagination is
running away with him. Were he to put such a thing in an under-
graduate essay today, his tutor would put a red line through it and
write 'NO!' in the margin. Alas, however, he had a huge impact on the
Church's teaching about this story and about Mary of Magdala (see
how she is commonly depicted in Western art), and the confusion
and nastiness introduced by his words have still not gone away.

Luke's calling the woman in Simon's house 'a sinner' does not nec-
essarily mean she is a prostitute at all. Earlier in his Gospel he tells of
Jesus calling Peter to follow him and has Peter say, 'Go away from me,
Lord, for I am a sinful man!' (Luke 5.8). The Greek word he uses there
is exactly the same as the one he applies to the woman in 7.37 and
again in 7.39. Yet, as Barbara Reid comments, 'commentators never
discuss what might be the type of sins Simon Peter has committed'.[4]
And no one at all, to my knowledge or even in my imagining, has suggested Peter was once a prostitute! Simon the Pharisee does not react
in the story as if the woman is a prostitute. He does not say to himself, 'How dare she burst into my dinner party and start plying her
filthy trade among my guests!' He simply criticizes her for 'touching'
Jesus. Klyne Snodgrass explains, 'Pharisees had a concern for purity
at meals that we can hardly appreciate.'[5] What the nature of the woman's 'sin' was we do not know, and Luke never enlightens us. Simon
sees her as unclean, as polluting those she touched and disturbing the
ritual purity of the meal. For his part Jesus will tell Simon the woman's sins have been many. That is all we have.

Luke remains unnervingly quick, however, to tell us she is 'a sinner', and that judgement sets up the controversy between Simon and
Jesus, an argument that will take over most of the rest of the story.
Many of these one-sceners in the Gospels get Jesus into such argument with his opponents and become sidelined in the process. In
this case, however, the woman is not so quickly ignored. Jesus takes
Simon to task:

Jesus spoke up and said to him, 'Simon, I have something to say to
you.' 'Teacher,' he replied, 'Speak.' 'A certain creditor had two debtors;

one owed five hundred denarii, and the other fifty. When they could not pay, he cancelled the debts for both of them. Now which of them will love him more?' Simon answered, 'I suppose the one for whom he cancelled the greater debt.' And Jesus said to him, 'You have judged rightly.' Then turning towards the woman, he said to Simon, 'Do you see this woman? I entered your house; you gave me no water for my feet, but she has bathed my feet with her tears and dried them with her hair. You gave me no kiss, but from the time I came in she has not stopped kissing my feet. You did not anoint my head with oil, but she has anointed my feet with ointment. Therefore, I tell you, her sins, which were many, have been forgiven; hence she has shown great love. But the one to whom little is forgiven, loves little.' Then he said to her, 'Your sins are forgiven.'   (7.40–48)

Jesus' long speech is addressed to Simon. Only at the very end does he speak to the woman. But everything he says is about her. Of course, it is about Simon, too, for he is the one who has been 'forgiven little', presumably because he thinks he has little need of forgiveness. He is the one who 'loves little', who does not love Jesus enough, as indeed in Luke's telling he has already revealed. When Jesus arrived he did not bring him water for him to wash his feet, greet him with a kiss or anoint his head. Surely these omissions amount not just to carelessness, discourtesy or lack of hospitality, but to insult. Yet Jesus' attention is primarily on the woman. He is more moved by her love than angry with Simon for his affront.

No wonder! Her courtesies are so extravagant! She has gone to a great deal of trouble. She has brought with her an alabaster jar of ointment. Alabaster was an expensive material, and the 'ointment' in Luke's Greek is myrrh, that same precious, fragrant resin as the magi bring to the infant Jesus in Matthew 2.11, when they present him with gifts they deem fit for a king. Myrrh is an important ingredient in the sacred anointing oil used in Exodus 30.23–32 for the consecration of priests, the tent of meeting, the ark of the covenant, the altars and the rest. With myrrh we enter the Holy of Holies. But myrrh is also mentioned as many as seven times in the passionate love poetry of the Song of Songs, and that is the clue to its use in this story. The woman has chosen her 'ointment' carefully. She is clearly rich to have been able to afford it, and its alabaster jar, too. Hers is plainly an extravagant gift, which to Jesus, at least, speaks of the extravagance of her love, as clearly as her tears and all her kisses, and her washing his feet.

We will return to the act of footwashing in the next chapter and the last, but a few things about it need to be said here. The washing of feet was a routine act, performed when you entered a house, including your own, and especially before a meal. Most people washed their own feet. Coming from a small, poor village in the Galilee hills, Jesus would never have had his feet washed, except by his mother when he was very small. Even in Simon's house he is expected to wash them himself: 'you gave me no water for my feet,' he says. The rich, however, had slaves to wash their feet for them, and those slaves were the 'tweenies' of their day, the young slave-girls at the very bottom of the domestic pile. Did this rich woman normally have her feet washed by a young slave? Quite possibly. Even if she did not, the significance of her washing someone's feet for them would hardly have been lost on her. It is an extraordinary thing to do. She casts all status and honour as a rich woman to the winds. 'By letting her hair down, touching Jesus' feet even with her hair, and anointing his feet with perfume she contravened every social convention of the day,' says Snodgrass. That is surely true. Alas, he adds, 'Were it not for her tears, the acts would border on the obscene.'[6] *Obscene?* It seems he has the nonsense of Gregory the Great ringing in his ears, has taken too much notice of that pesky word 'sinner' and paid too much attention to the judgement of Simon the Pharisee. Because Simon's judgement is not Luke's, nor that of Jesus. In their view, and it is Jesus' that counts, of course, her actions are ones of pure love.

But why does this woman love Jesus so? Jesus himself supplies the answer. She loves much because she has been forgiven much. Now we can understand why she wanted to know where Jesus was and has come to the meal. This is not the first time she has met Jesus. The story makes no sense if it is. How many times she has met him already we cannot know, for Luke does not describe their first encounter(s), telling us only that she had found herself forgiven. In Jesus' company she was no longer a sinner. She was a child of God, a member of God's family. She was accepted, acceptable. No longer did she risk polluting others. They did not have to beware of her touching them. With Jesus she found a new dignity and a new love, as large as the love of God. And so, overwhelmed with her own love for Jesus, she takes up her precious jar of myrrh and goes to where she has heard he is eating, not to join in the meal but to act as his slave.

In that case why does Jesus need to say to her, 'Your sins are forgiven'? Because Simon and his other guests need to hear it. They need to stop calling her 'a sinner' and instead recognize her as a devoted friend of Jesus, a person forgiven, accepted, embraced, shining with the mercy of God. The woman's new status needs to go public and be acknowledged by all; otherwise she cannot resume her rightful place in that devout community.

Tragically they fail to acknowledge it. 'But those who were at the table with him began to say among themselves, "Who is this who even forgives sins?" ' (7.49). Good question, but Jesus will not allow himself to be drawn into further argument. 'And he said to the woman, "Your faith has saved you; go in peace" ' (7.50). These words, together with 'Your sins are forgiven', are the only ones Jesus addresses to the woman, and Luke does not tell us her response. In the whole passage we never hear her voice, for with Jesus' 'go in peace' the story ends, and we never hear of this woman again.

Or perhaps, perhaps we do. The very next passage in Luke's narrative goes like this:

> Soon afterwards he went on through cities and villages, proclaiming and bringing the good news of the kingdom of God. The twelve were with him, as well as some women who had been cured of evil spirits and infirmities: Mary, called Magdalene, from whom seven demons had gone out, and Joanna, the wife of Herod's steward Chuza, and Susanna, and many others, who provided for them out of their resources. (8.1–3)

In our Bibles these words begin a new chapter, but we should remember that is not of Luke's doing. The chapter divisions so familiar to us were introduced into the Latin Bible by Stephen Langton, a lecturer at the University of Paris and later Archbishop of Canterbury, who died in 1228. In truth 8.1–3 is more obviously linked with the story of the woman anointing Jesus than with what follows, the parables of The Sower and The Lamp under a Jar. One could argue the chapter division is misplaced and would fit better between 8.3 and 8.4. Verses 1–3 do not represent an introduction to the parables so much as a conclusion to the story of the anointing. When we see them as that, we find ourselves asking whether we should include the woman in Simon's house among those who followed Jesus from place to place, among the 'many other' women, 'who provided for them out of their own resources' (the grammar of Luke's Greek makes plain the 'many others' were all women).

Luke does not allow us to answer that question with any certainty, but his narrative leaves us with a few clues. Why should he insert the mention of those other women followers *immediately* after the story of the anointing? In describing them as providing for Jesus and his entourage out of their own resources, he is talking of women who between them had considerable funds at their disposal. As Richard Bauckham says, 'Luke is not telling his readers that the women cooked the meals, washed the dishes, and mended the clothes.'[7] They were able to support Jesus' ministry financially and give him the freedom to pursue it in the way he wished. We have already remarked that the woman who anoints Jesus in Simon's house is wealthy. She is also an outsider, or has been treated as such by her community. She has, it seems, no husband. She is either unmarried, or more likely her husband is dead or has divorced her. She appears to have no ties, but she does have money. As such she has the opportunity to up and follow Jesus and to contribute to the common fund. And she has the motive, also, of course. Jesus has changed her life. With Jesus she belongs, and to him she is utterly devoted. The story in the house ends with Jesus saying to her 'go in peace'. That might seem to point in the other direction and effectively remove her from the continuing narrative. But it is not as clear as that. Later in chapter 8, when a man who calls himself Legion is healed by Jesus, he begs to go with him. To him Jesus replies, 'Return to your home, and declare how much God has done for you' (8.39). The words addressed to the woman are much less precise.

If she does follow Jesus, then Luke would have us picture her at the cross and among the women who first discover the empty tomb and stumble upon Jesus' resurrection. Luke concludes his account of the crucifixion with the words, 'But all his acquaintances, including the women who had followed him from Galilee, stood at a distance, watching these things' (23.49). And when the women rush back from the tomb to the others with their extraordinary news, he explains, 'Now it was Mary Magdalene, Joanna, Mary the mother of James, and the other women with them who told this to the apostles' (24.10).

This is the trouble with the one-sceners in the Gospels. They appear almost out of nowhere and then they disappear, or appear to do so, leaving so many questions unanswered. Sometimes, as in this case, they leave a few clues behind them, but that is unusual. Make no mistake, Luke has written a magnificent story here, but he does not tell us enough about the woman's situation and her experience before it begins, or about how she expressed her commitment to Jesus after it ends. Within the story itself we never learn the woman's name, nor do we hear her voice. Most of the passage is made up of dialogue, but it is dialogue about her, not with her. At no point is she given anything to say for herself. Her actions speak louder than words, we might say. But this woman has been empowered by Jesus, and finding a voice and having it heard and heeded belong to empowerment, to hers as much as to anyone else's. Her silence is one of the shadows of this story. She seems as deeply devoted to Jesus as any other figure we meet in the pages of Luke's Gospel, at least beyond the infancy narratives of the first two chapters. Yet her experience of forgiveness, her love for Jesus and her continuing commitment to him are too large to be contained in these few verses. She is a changed woman. That much is clear. But how that continues to play out in *her* story is not. There are hints here of a gospel stretching beyond the Gospel.

A different anointing

When we turn to Mark's and Matthew's versions of the anointing of Jesus, we find ourselves dealing essentially with another story. An unnamed woman anoints Jesus using an alabaster jar of expensive perfume during a meal at the house of a man called Simon, and her actions lead to controversy. All this, of course, belongs to Luke's story as well. But there the similarities end.

Simon is a leper in Mark and Matthew, not a Pharisee, and he is not the one who initiates the argument with Jesus. Once Matthew has introduced the story by saying, 'Now while Jesus was at Bethany in the house of Simon the leper', this Simon plays no further part at all. He cannot even be called a one-scener. He has but a single verse to his name. Neither Matthew nor Mark begins to tell the larger story of his encounter(s) with Jesus.

Normally in examining such a text we would start with Mark, not Matthew, since Mark's Gospel was composed first and Matthew used him as one of his main sources. However, in this case Mark's Greek has its problems. Morna Hooker describes it as 'full of awkward Greek phrases that look very much like clumsy translations from Aramaic'.[8] So we will lay out Matthew's text, and point out in our discussion where Mark agrees or disagrees with it.

> Now while Jesus was at Bethany in the house of Simon the leper, a woman came to him with an alabaster jar of very costly ointment, and she poured it on his head as he sat at the table. But when the disciples saw it, they were angry and said, 'Why this waste? For this ointment could have been sold for a large sum, and the money given to the poor.' But Jesus, aware of this, said to them, 'Why do you trouble the woman? She has performed a good service for me. For you always have the poor with you, but you will not always have me. By pouring this ointment on my body she has prepared me for burial. Truly I tell you, wherever this good news is proclaimed in the whole world, what she has done will be told in remembrance of her.' (Matthew 26.6–13)

Matthew has abbreviated Mark's version somewhat. His Greek describes 'the ointment' simply as *muros*, or myrrh, the same as in Luke. Mark has a cumbersome phrase: 'a woman came with an alabaster jar of very costly ointment [*muros*] of nard', where 'myrrh' seems to be what it sometimes is, the generic word for perfume. However,

Mark's bringing the words 'nard' and 'myrrh' together draws us to verses near the beginning of the Song of Songs:

> While the king was on his couch,
>   my nard gave forth its fragrance.
> My beloved is to me a bag of myrrh
>   that lies between my breasts.
>   (Song of Songs 1.12–13)

We cannot catch that particular echo in Matthew's simpler text. Nor do we hear the voice of the woman, as we do in the Song of Songs.[9] In both Mark and Matthew, as in Luke, she remains mute, and we almost lose sight of her in the swirling clouds of anger her action provokes. Matthew says it is the disciples who get angry. Mark leaves it vague: 'But some were there who said to one another in anger'. In each case these are blind to what the woman has done. 'Do you see this woman?' Jesus asks in Luke's story. He might well have asked the same in Matthew and Mark. Those who 'trouble the woman' (Matthew 26.10) or 'scold' her (Mark 14.5) are not concerned about her at all, but only with how expensive her perfume is. They say in Mark it was worth 'more than three hundred denarii' (Mark 14.5), which is equivalent to a whole year's wage for a labourer. She smashes her alabaster jar, Mark tells us, and pours the perfume all over Jesus. As John the Baptist pours water over Jesus' head to signal the start of his public ministry, so here the woman pours lavish quantities of perfume over his head to mark the beginning of his Passion. And all the disciples or Jesus' fellow guests can say is, 'What a waste!' It is shocking, and Mark and Matthew mean us to find it so. Their comment at the end of the passage makes that clear.

Immediately before his version of the story Mark tells us, 'The chief priests and the scribes were looking for a way to arrest Jesus by stealth and kill him' (Mark 14.1b). Matthew has something very similar. But this is not the first time these Evangelists have spoken of Jesus' coming death. Three times each of them has had Jesus tell his disciples that he is going to be executed (Mark 8.31, 9.31, 10.33–34; Matthew 16.21, 17.22–23, 20.17–19). This makes Matthew's version, with his identifying the disciples as the woman's detractors, the more startling of the two. The woman recognizes what the disciples consistently refuse to do, that Jesus must die, and must die soon. Furthermore, Jesus has made it quite plain that he will die the death of a criminal. The woman understands the implications. It will not be possible to anoint Jesus' body for burial after he dies, for the corpse of an executed criminal was not usually released to the family. Only after a year would they receive the bones and be able to bury them. Mark's or Matthew's Jesus could have added another to his question in Luke: 'Do you see what this woman sees?' She is clear-sighted. She knows the times, and being practical she seizes the moment. In Luke her counterpart is driven by love. Here, in Mark and Matthew, that same love flows over with grief.

She also knows who Jesus is. In Homer's great epic poem, *The Odyssey*, Odysseus returns home disguised as a beggar after 20 years' fighting at Troy. In a famous scene his old nurse, Eurycleia, then washes his feet. As she cradles his leg and passes her hands down it she feels an old scar, the unmistakable mark of a wound Odysseus sustained as a boy.

> She felt it, knew it, suddenly let his foot fall –
> down it dropped in the basin – the bronze clanged,
> tipping over, spilling water across the floor.
> Joy and torment gripped her heart at once,
> tears rushed to her eyes – voice choked in her throat
> she reached for Odysseus' chin and whispered quickly,
> 'Yes, yes! you are *Odysseus* – oh dear boy –
> I couldn't know you before . . .
> not till I touched the body of my king!'
>
> (*The Odyssey*, 19.530–538)[10]

The woman in the house of Simon the leper also supposes she touches the body of her king. Hers is no recognition scene, however. She does not discover Jesus' identity as she anoints him. She has come prepared with her jar of perfume because she has already found him as her Messiah, Israel's longed-for king, and knows he will receive no proper coronation. He will be hailed 'King of the Jews' (Mark 15.18; Matthew 27.29), but in bitter mockery, and a cross will be his throne and sharp thorns his crown. As Samuel, the prophet, anointed David king (1 Samuel 16.13), so she comes to the meal as Jesus' prophet. Alone of Jesus' coronation ceremonies, hers is done with love and not with fear and hate.

Almost immediately after the anointing both Mark and Matthew tell of Jesus eating the Passover meal with his disciples, and there he talks of his 'body' and his 'blood', of his offering himself up as the

Passover lamb that will make this particular festival like no other. But to make sacrifice, even to sacrifice himself, Jesus must be a priest. So the woman anoints him as priest also, or rather, her extravagant act of anointing signifies her recognition of his priesthood.

> How very good and pleasant it is
>   when kindred live together in unity!
> It is like the precious oil on the head,
>   running down upon the beard,
> on the beard of Aaron,
> running down over the collar of his robes.
>   (Psalm 133.1–2)

'You shall take the anointing-oil, and pour it on his head and anoint him' (Exodus 29.7). Thus Moses is instructed by God, when he is about to ordain his brother Aaron priest. The woman is Jesus' prophet, his Samuel, and she is his Moses. She has made him ready.

As Jesus says in this story, she has 'performed a good service' or as we might put it, if we were to translate that clause in Mark 14.6 and Matthew 26.10 more literally, she has 'done a fine deed'. He can go on now towards his death, the death that will change everything. Is not this one of the most astonishing, most daring, most radical passages in all the Gospels? Mark and Matthew both suggest it is. They put a final word in Jesus' mouth that must surely have originated with them as they sought through their writings to bring the story of Jesus to a wider world: 'Truly I tell you, wherever the good news is proclaimed in the whole world, what she has done will be told in remembrance of her' (Mark 14.9; Matthew 26.13 is almost identical).

And we do not even know what to call her. We know Samuel's name. We know Moses' name. We know the name of Odysseus' old nurse, Eurycleia. Ched Myers, in his commentary on Mark, makes a virtue out of the woman's anonymity, and suggests she stands for all those women who showed their grasp of the heart of Jesus' teaching in their service, and their devotion to him in their ability to endure the cross.[11] Maybe that is so, but I cannot help thinking Myers has tried to make the story better than it is. For it is not just the woman's name that is kept from us. We have already noticed that she is given nothing to say. And like the woman in Luke 7, she must have previous. This cannot be the first time she has encountered Jesus. She knows who he is; she knows the significance of the time. She has a wisdom and an understanding that the male disciples lack, though they have been following Jesus all this time, through Galilee and now to Jerusalem. She must surely have been following Jesus herself. Her story makes no sense otherwise. Does not this one scene present her as an exemplary, true, faithful disciple? In the fine words they put into the mouth of Jesus at the end of the passage Mark and Matthew both go out of their way to do her justice.

Yet we cannot say they succeed. Not only do they fail to give her any words to say, they do not tell of any addressed to her, either. Her detractors speak among themselves, and even Jesus does not address her. He speaks to those who trouble or scold her. He says nothing to her, and then it is too late: the story is ended and the narrative moves on to Judas Iscariot and his betrayal. Mark and Matthew have packed an enormous amount into a few remarkable verses, but they leave a larger story untold, an even brighter gospel beyond their Gospels. In her seminal work, *In Memory of Her*, Elizabeth Fiorenza points out the results of their omission:

> In the passion account of Mark's Gospel three disciples figure prominently: on the one hand, two of the twelve – Judas who betrays Jesus and Peter who denies him – and on the other, the unnamed woman who anoints Jesus. But while the stories of Judas and Peter are engraved in the memory of Christians, the story of the woman is virtually forgotten . . . Even her name is lost to us. Wherever the gospel is proclaimed and the eucharist celebrated another story is told: the story of the apostle who betrayed Jesus.[12]

In the next chapter we will examine John's handling of the anointing story.

Living among the dead

In Mark, Matthew and Luke most of the one-sceners are people who are healed by Jesus. There is a veritable host of them. We will spend the rest of this chapter focusing on a single one, the man who calls himself Legion. We have already mentioned Luke's story about him, but in our discussion we will concentrate on Mark.

In the Gospels Jesus spends almost all his time among his fellow Jews. Occasionally, however, we find him in Gentile territory, and that is the case in Mark 5.1–20. Mark's previous passage describes Jesus sailing over the Sea of Galilee with his disciples, from the Jewish shore on the west to Gentile territory on the east (4.35–41). In Mark's hands it is no ordinary crossing. A huge storm arises, the boat is on the point of sinking, and Jesus' friends fear they will soon drown. Yet that is not the half of it. Mark's story is heavy with symbolism, with ancient myth and with the poetry of the Old Testament. In the midst of the storm Jesus is asleep, a tiny pocket of calm in the centre of the maelstrom and the disciples' terror. When the disciples wake him, he 'rebukes' the wind and commands the sea. 'Be quiet! Hold your peace!' he says, or in a more literal translation of the second Greek verb, 'Be muzzled!' At once the wind falls 'exhausted' and there is a flat calm (the NRSV's 'Then the wind ceased' is too prosaic) (4.39).

Mark's language is highly poetic and very particular. He pictures the wind and storm as malevolent beasts, out to destroy Jesus and his companions. He calls to mind the ancient myth, long widespread in the ancient Near East, of a titanic struggle between the creator gods and a great sea monster. In that myth the monster embodies the forces of evil and chaos that threaten to undo the gods' work. Against that background the poets of the Old Testament celebrate their God's victory over evil and the triumph of hope by telling of his stilling a storm-wracked sea or trampling on the sea's back. 'You rule the raging of the sea,' they cry. 'When its waves rise, you still them' (Psalm 89.9).

> When the waters saw you, O God,
>   when the waters saw you, they were afraid;
> the very deep trembled.   (Psalm 77.16)

Sometimes, when the forces of evil appear to have the upper hand, the poets accuse God of being asleep and call on him to wake up:

Awake, awake, put on strength,
O arm of the LORD!
(Isaiah 51.9)

Psalm 107 has it thus:

Then they cried to the LORD in their trouble,
and he brought them out from their distress;
he made the storm be still,
and the waves of the sea were hushed.
Then they were glad because they had quiet,
and he brought them to their desired haven.
(vv. 28–30)

With these words in our heads we know where we are when we make the far shore in what Mark calls the country of the Gerasenes. His geography seems rather muddled, but that does not matter. We know we are in the presence of one who has just shown us God and his ancient power over the forces of chaos. He brings with him the kingdom of God, where all is well and all manner of things can be well. He has God's authority and God's determination to make all things new.

As soon as he lands, Jesus needs all the power and authority he has just displayed. 'Immediately,' Mark tells us – he is fond of 'immediately'; it adds to the pace of his narrative – 'a man out of the tombs with an unclean spirit met him' (5.2). So begins what is the longest and most detailed healing story in the whole of his Gospel, and Mark devotes what is for him a surprising amount of time to describing the man.

He lived among the tombs; and no one could restrain him any more, even with a chain; for he had often been restrained with shackles and chains, but the chains he wrenched apart, and the shackles he broke in pieces; and no one had the strength to subdue him. Night and day among the tombs and on the mountains he was always howling and bruising himself with stones. When he saw Jesus from a distance, he ran and bowed down before him; and he shouted at the top of his voice, 'What have you to do with me, Jesus, Son of the Most High God? I adjure you by God, do not torment me.' For he had said to him, 'Come out of the man, you unclean spirit!' Then Jesus asked him, 'What is your name?' He replied, 'My name is Legion; for we are many.' He begged him earnestly not to send them out of the country. Now there on the hillside a great herd of swine was feeding; and the unclean spirits begged him, 'Send us into the swine; let us enter them.' So he

gave them permission. And the unclean spirits came out and entered
the swine; and the herd, numbering about two thousand, rushed down
the steep bank into the lake, and were drowned in the lake.   (5.3–13)

The spotlight is turned on this poor man and held there, and we hear
his voice, also, both his fearful howling and the words he addresses to
Jesus. The disciples are there, but they remain invisible and inaudible.
They will never make their presence felt in this story. It is between
Jesus and the man – though some swineherds and the people of the
area will make an appearance in the second half.

Why does Mark pay this man such close attention? The quick
answer is this: by emphasizing his desperate condition he can make
plain the unique authority of the one who heals him. In other words
he paints his dramatic picture of the man in order to further exalt
Jesus. Well, of course he does. Honouring Jesus is what Mark's Gospel
is about. Yet let us give Mark his due here. We do not have to go
searching for clues about this man, sifting through the details of the
narrative to see what we can find or can properly imagine. Mark tells
us, and tells us plainly.

When next in Mark Jesus crosses the Sea of Galilee and enters
Gentile territory, the reception he gets will be very different. That
crossing will again be remarkable, for Jesus will come to his disciples,
straining at the oars against a strong wind, walking on the surface of
the water (6.47–52).

> Your way was through the sea,
>> your path, through the mighty waters;
>> yet your footprints were unseen.

So says the Psalmist in Psalm 77.19, and Job refers to God as the one

> who alone stretched out the heavens
> and trampled the waves of the Sea.
> (Job 9.8)

The wind of that second crossing again falls 'exhausted' (Mark
uses the same Greek verb in 6.51 as in 4.39), but this time when
they reach land the calm remains. The dark forces for the time being
are beaten.

> [T]hey came to land at Gennesaret and moored the boat. When they
> got out of the boat, people at once recognized him, and rushed about
> that whole region and began to bring the sick on mats to wherever

they heard he was. And wherever he went, into villages or cities or farms, they laid the sick in the market-places, and begged him that they might touch even the fringe of his cloak; and all who touched it were healed.   (6.53b–56)

Jesus is visibly Jewish. As a Torah-observing Jew he is wearing tassels on the corners of his garment. Mark uses the term *kraspedon* for what the NRSV translates as 'fringe', and it is the same word we find in the Greek Septuagint version of Numbers 15.38, 39, when it talks of the tassels Jewish males must wear to remind them of the Torah and its demands. Orthodox Jewish men and boys still wear them today. It is these Jewish tassels the sick among the Gentiles on the eastern side of the Sea of Galilee reach out for; they touch them and are healed.

When Jesus reaches Gentile territory for the first time, however, in Mark 4, it is as if the storm has not abated at all but is raging still, with all its ancient ferocity, all its fearful destructiveness, but now within the confines of the mind and body of a man. In the most daring description of the forces of chaos and evil in all Scripture, where they are pictured as a great beast called Behemoth, or a dragon named Leviathan, the poet of the book of Job has God declare that he himself must approach Behemoth with sword drawn (40.19b). He asks Job a series of questions designed to emphasize Leviathan's strength and terror:

> Can you draw out Leviathan with a fishhook,
>   or press down its tongue with a cord?
> Can you put a rope in its nose,
>   or pierce its jaw with a hook?
> Will it make many supplications to you?
>   Will it speak soft words to you?
> Will it make a covenant with you
>   to be taken as your servant for ever?
> Will you play with it as with a bird,
>   or will you put it on a leash for your girls?
>   (Job 41.1–5)

Like these ancient mythic beasts in Job, the man who confronts Jesus has proved already, time and time again, that he cannot be tamed or domesticated. The local people have tried to control him with chains and shackles round his ankles, but to no avail. He is dangerous and violent, with the physical strength of a Samson or Hercules. And Jesus has no sword to draw. The disciples are present, but it is as if they are not there. To all intents and purposes Jesus is alone with this man and his veritable legion of demons.

All those healed by Jesus in the Gospels are to one extent or another isolated from their families and their communities. We all wish to belong, and for us in the West, in the twenty-first century, loneliness can be terrible. But anthropologists and sociologists agree that in the first-century Mediterranean world the focus was much less on the individual and individual goals than on the group and its well-being. To be outside one's group was to be counted more dead than alive. In Jewish society a person declared unclean through contracting what is translated in our Bibles as leprosy, for example, had to leave the community. 'He shall live alone,' says Leviticus 13.46; 'his dwelling shall be outside the camp.' In 'group-orientated societies, such excommunication is devastating. It is the equivalent of a death sentence,' says John Pilch in his book *Healing in the New Testament*.[13]

The man in Mark 5 is a Gentile, and from a Jewish perspective already an outsider. His particular situation marks him out for the Jew as totally unclean. When Isaiah wishes to denounce his own people and describe how far they have gone away from God, he talks of those,

> who sit inside tombs,
>   and spend the night in secret places;
> who eat swine's flesh.   (Isaiah 65.4)

Mark does not tell of the man eating pork, but he lives among pigs and among the dead. And he is, of course, an outsider in his own community as well. He has no community, beyond that of his demons and the dead. 'It is the equivalent of a death sentence,' says Pilch. 'He lived among the tombs,' says Mark. No one else in all the Gospels is as isolated as this man. He reminds us of the most tragic stories to have come out in recent years from the African countries ravaged by Ebola, accounts of those contracting the virus or surviving it being cut off from their families and their communities, surrounded only by fear.

The man is naked, as we learn later in the story where we find him fully clothed, and that for the hearers and readers of Mark's Gospel would have been a further source of shame. Not surprisingly some of his rages are turned against himself. He beats and cuts himself with stones. Already torturing himself, he begs Jesus not to torture him further ('torment' in 5.7 would better be translated 'torture'). Sometimes we seem to hear him speaking; sometimes it is the dark forces within him. 'What have you to do with me?' he asks Jesus. 'I adjure you by God, do not torture me.' Yet when Jesus asks his name, he replies, 'My name is Legion; for we are many.' His name is not Legion. That is not the name he was given when he was born, the name his family and village knew him by as he grew up. It is the name of his demons. As Ched Myers comments, the word 'legion' means only one thing in Mark's world: a division of Roman soldiers.[14] So the name reminded the first-century Christians, as they listened to a performance of Mark's Gospel, of the Roman Empire in which they lived and the means its rulers used to assert and reassert their power. It added its own resonance to the distant place he must have occupied in their minds, enlarged their sense of his otherness. Legion is not a good name to have.

The man is in complete chaos. One moment he is bowing down before Jesus as if he is worshipping him, the next he is yelling at him at the top of his voice. He knows full well who he is. The woman at Bethany also knows, but her knowledge is that of a quiet, deep wisdom. The man's recognizing Jesus as the 'Son of the Most High God' comes out of his madness and its supernatural roots (as Mark would have explained it, with his talk of demons or unclean spirits). One moment the man is begging Jesus not to send him out of the region, the next his demons are pleading with him to send them into the pigs. If they think the pigs will be a safe place for them to hide, they are, of course, mistaken.

With the drowning of the pigs and the return of the demons to the depths of the sea, where the great sea dragon of the ancient myth dwells, the first scene of the story ends. We have seen an army of demons and 2,000 pigs; now, in the second and final scene, we find some swineherds and a crowd of people:

> The swineherds ran off and told it in the city and in the country. Then people came to see what it was that had happened. They came to Jesus and saw the demoniac sitting there, clothed and in his right mind, the very man who had had the legion; and they were afraid. Those who had seen what had happened to the demoniac and to the swine reported it. Then they began to beg Jesus to leave their neighbourhood. As he was getting into the boat, the man who had been possessed by demons

begged him that he might be with him. But Jesus refused, and said to him, 'Go home to your friends, and tell them how much the Lord has done for you, and what mercy he has shown you.' And he went away and began to proclaim in the Decapolis how much Jesus had done for him; and everyone was amazed. (5.14–20)

We do not lose sight here of the man Jesus has healed. There he is still, centre stage with Jesus, 'clothed and in his right mind'. Why are the people so afraid? Why do they beg Jesus to leave their shores? Ched Myers interprets the whole story as a symbolic tale. 'The demon (*sic*) ... represents,' he suggests,

> Roman military power. In the symbolic act of exorcism, the legion 'begged him ... earnestly not to send them out of the country'! Nor is it surprising that there would be worried opposition to such an 'expulsion' from the residents of the Decapolis, given the concrete experience of the Roman scorched-earth campaign of reconquest.[15]

This turns the man among the tombs into a symbol, and robs him of the humanity which Mark is so careful to give him. Whatever else Mark is doing here, he is meaning us to engage with a human being in a desperate plight, who, as a result of his encounter with Jesus, finds again his humanity, who is given dignity and peace, a highly significant piece of work to do, a renewed sense of belonging and an end to his great loneliness. Mark himself provides another explanation for the people's fear, in his conclusion to his tale of the stilling of the storm, in words that fall immediately before the start of the healing story: 'And they were filled with great awe and said to one another, "Who then is this, that even the wind and the sea obey him?" ' (4.41).

'And they were filled with great awe', as the NRSV has it, could be translated more literally, 'they feared a great fear'. It is the deep, unsettling, holy fear that commonly overtakes people in the Bible when they come within touching distance of the divine. It overtakes Moses at the Burning Bush: 'And Moses hid his face, for he was afraid to look upon God' (Exodus 3.6). Later in Mark it will overcome Peter, James and John on the mountain of the Transfiguration (Mark 9.6), and the women who stumble upon Jesus' resurrection (16.8). Of Moses at the Burning Bush I once wrote, 'Suddenly the reality, the closeness of God is too much to bear.'[16] So now the people of Mark 5, looking at the man sitting calmly among them, and hearing what has happened to the pigs and the demons, suddenly find the closeness of God too much to bear and send Jesus away.

And Jesus begins to get into the boat. But if our eyes are still fixed on the man who has been healed, we cry, 'But Jesus cannot leave now! What of the man left behind?' Healing in the Mediterranean world of the first century always involved the ties of community being restored. At the point in the story when Jesus is getting back into the boat, the man is still isolated. He is still surrounded by the fear of the local people, as he was at the start. His healing is not yet complete. Jesus surely cannot leave now. The man himself makes sure Jesus turns back. He begs to go with him. How do we hear his plea? Is he asking to become a disciple and follower of the one who has shown him God? Or is he desperate to join the 'family' of Jesus and his disciples, because he has nowhere else to go? Or both? Mark does not allow us to get inside his mind, but if the man believes he has nowhere else to go, then he is mistaken. 'Go home to your friends,' Jesus tells him, or rather, 'Depart to your home and to your own' – a more literal translation of Mark's Greek. 'Your own' is stronger than 'your friends', and wider in its reference. It includes his family, his extended family and his former community. 'They are *yours*,' Jesus tells him. At the start of the story he had no community to call his own, except for the terrifying force of his demons and the shadowy presence of other people's ancestors. Back home, he will belong once again. His healing will be complete. And his family and community will be healed also. His being restored to them will be their restoration. With his chaos banished, their order can be renewed.

'And he went away and began to proclaim in the Decapolis how much Jesus had done for him; and everyone was amazed.' So ends his story. Except it doesn't, not quite. For when Jesus next crosses over to the eastern side of the Sea of Galilee, he is besieged, as we have already seen, by people coming to him for healing (6.53–56). This is the first time in the narrative that Jesus has returned to what Mark calls 'the far side' of the Sea of Galilee since the man's healing. (Mark's geography is again confused, for Gennesaret was on the western side of the lake, south of Capernaum, but no matter.) 'And everyone was amazed.' Now in 6.53–56 we can see the full extent of their amazement and just how much the healed man has achieved!

We learn much more in this particular story about the person healed than we do in most of the other healing stories in the Gospels.

And yet we still do not know what to call him. 'Legion' will not do. If we still have any doubt about that, we must remind ourselves of how Mark describes him in the second scene: 'the man who had had the legion' (5.15). And if Legion was not his real name at the start, it is entirely inappropriate at the finish.

Furthermore, there are the questions of the man's previous history and of his subsequent life. Unlike the woman or women who anoint Jesus, this man has not encountered Jesus before. He recognizes him when he gets out of the boat, not because he has already met him, but because his demons have supernatural insight: they see clearly the threat that Jesus poses to them. To borrow a vivid image from Luke, they can see Satan falling from heaven (see Luke 10.18) and the kingdom of God being established in his place. In the very first of his healing miracles Mark has an unclean spirit call out, 'What have you to do with us, Jesus of Nazareth? Have you come to destroy us? I know who you are, the Holy One of God' (Mark 1.24). So this time we do not have to imagine a previous meeting to make sense of the story. But though the story itself may not have its own history in that sense, the man does. What brought him to living among the dead in such a fearful state? What are the origins of his rage and his violence? Is the clue in that word 'legion'? Should we think the man has witnessed or experienced Roman brutality and torture? James Dunn recommends caution. He acknowledges 'the typically ruthless Roman suppression' of the uprising of Galilean insurgents after the death in 4 BC of Herod the Great. He reminds us that the Galilean city of Sepphoris was captured and burnt, and its inhabitants enslaved, and that conflict would 'no doubt have formed a major scar on the local consciousness for the generation following'. On the other hand he says, 'So long as taxes were paid and there was no undue unrest, the ruling hand of Rome was fairly light.' Even in Judea and Jerusalem the Roman military presence was small. 'For Galilee during the whole of Jesus' life there the fact of Roman rule would be, for the most part, even less obtrusive . . . the Romans were *not* an army of occupation.'[17] The messages, therefore, are mixed, and we cannot safely hang too much on the name the man gives his demons. Yet it is the only possible clue Mark gives us. The rest is silence. Surely the man must have been caught up in some great catastrophe in his previous life. But we cannot say more than that without indulging in speculation.

On the subject of the man's life after his encounter with Jesus, however, Mark is clearer. We are left to imagine his return home, but we are told plainly he proclaimed in the Decapolis what Jesus had done for him. The Decapolis was a confederation of ten Greek cities lying for the most part east of the River Jordan, and though there were Jews living in the region, its population was largely Gentile. As we have already seen, the setting for the man's healing is plainly a Gentile one. Not only has Jesus crossed the Sea of Galilee to get there, but the place is swarming with pigs, animals that to Jews were unclean and unfit for food. The man himself addresses Jesus as 'Son of the Most High God', and 'the Most High God' is a title we find in several places in the Bible on the lips of Gentiles referring to the God of Israel (see Genesis 14.18–20; Numbers 24.16; Isaiah 14.14; Daniel 3.26, 4.2). This Gentile man becomes a disciple of Jesus. He does not join at any stage, as far as we are aware, the company of those who follow Jesus from place to place. And yet he is more than a disciple. He is an evangelist, a Gentile who brings the good news of Jesus to the Gentiles, the first such figure in Mark's Gospel. And those verses about Jesus' popularity in 6.53–56 suggest he does a remarkable job. Dennis Nineham, in his commentary on Mark, has his eye on this later passage as he writes about the story of the man's healing:

> This is the first time in the Gospel that Jesus has been in Gentile ter-ritory, so it is the more noteworthy that his holy presence routs and banishes uncleanness. In effect the land is cleansed by his coming, and the way prepared for its Christianizing, a task which, at the end of this story, Jesus explicitly lays upon the man previously possessed by the demons. The story may thus have been intended to explain how this predominantly Gentile area became a home for Christianity, and will also perhaps have provided support for the Gentile mission of the early Church.[18]

A matter of focus

It may seem as though my demands of the Gospel writers in this chapter have been unreasonable. Why should we expect Mark, Matthew or Luke to have addressed all the questions I have thrown at them about the woman who anoints Jesus' feet in Luke, the one who anoints his head in Matthew and Mark, or the man living among the dead? Their Gospels are about Jesus of Nazareth, after all, and if they had gone into the kind of detail I have been exploring about all their one-sceners, their books would have been impossibly long and too heavy to carry from one Christian community to the next, and, more importantly, would surely have lost their focus and their impact. Each Gospel is a life of Jesus, albeit a biography of an ancient and very particular kind. It is not a collection of biographies of a host of people gathered round a central figure.

Yet I do not think it is quite as simple as that. Each Evangelist meant to honour Jesus, to proclaim him as the one 'who shows us God',[19] the one who establishes the realm of God, where the ancient hopes of Israel, and indeed of the whole world, are fulfilled, most especially the hopes and longings of those who are ignored, despised, excluded. They included elements of his teaching, and they told stories of what happened to him, particularly how he came to be arrested, tried and killed, and then how he slipped out of death clothed in divinity. But along the way they told a host of stories of individuals he met and whose lives he transformed. In these stories, too, they set out to honour Jesus. Might they have honoured him more if they had shone the light more brightly on these individuals, held the light in place for a little longer, and thus demonstrated more clearly just how much honour Jesus bestowed on them? Might they have made an even greater impact, if they had explored a little more thoroughly just how much impact Jesus had on these people?

The extent of their explorations varies, it is true. The amount of detail Mark gives us about the man among the tombs is remarkable, but even there important questions about him remain. As for the woman who anoints Jesus' head in Matthew and Mark, we do not even know whether she was the same woman as anoints his feet in Luke. Did two women anoint Jesus, or was it only one? Was there just one occasion of Jesus' anointing or two, or indeed more than two?

And if it was only one woman, was she indeed Mary of Bethany, as John will tell us she was?

Behind such stories as these in the Gospels lie real events, real people. Jesus must, to say the very least, have paid them the very closest attention, for without that nothing would have happened and the stories would not have been told at all. Might the Evangelists have paid them similar attention, and done so consistently?

It is all a matter of focus.

2

'The Vikings were all men!'

A furious letter

Issue 74 of *Cam*, the Cambridge Alumni Magazine, contains an article by Lucy Jolin on the preservation of archaeological artefacts, in which she makes reference to the work of Dr Helen Geake, Visiting Scholar at the McDonald Institute for Archaeological Research. She concludes her article with a wonderful story about her:

> When Geake, a regular on Channel 4's *Time Team*, participated in a BBC television programme on early-medieval seafaring, the production company received a furious letter concerning the discussion on the role of women within Viking Society. 'This is a lie!' it read. 'The Vikings were all men!' It was funny, she says, but it illustrated a truth about preservation: we build our stories of the past simply on the accident of what's left behind.[1]

Soon after I read that article I was attending my local parish church when the lay person who led the intercessions referred to the Church having begun with 12 men. Her prayers were thoughtful and helpful, and I told her so after the service, on the way to coffee in the church hall. 'But what about the women?' I asked. 'Oh, women didn't count then,' she replied.

But women did count. Within the Judaism of the time they had more freedom and authority than Christians and even academic commentators have sometimes imagined. The Gospels themselves bear witness to that.[2] However, they also go some way to encourage the view that the Church began with 12 men, and such a narrative has been reinforced over and over again for 2,000 years by the Church's own teaching and preaching and by countless stained-glass windows, icons, paintings and frescoes. In the second century the Church put 'the Twelve' on high pedestals, and there they have remained ever since. 'The Vikings were all men!' said the furious letter-writer. 'The disciples were all men!' many still say and occasionally assert with similar strength of feeling. But it is not true. It is an ancient lie, put about by powerful men within the Church. If we look hard enough at the Gospels, we will recognize its falsity for ourselves. And we will see something more remarkable. A pattern will emerge where it is the women among the disciples of Jesus who truly grasp what his life and his teaching are about, while his male followers repeatedly show a shocking failure to understand. The male leaders of the Church have covered this up for too long. It is time to take off the wraps.

'Follow me'

In the first chapter we spoke of the impact Jesus made on those he met. Right from the start of his Gospel Mark lays it on with a trowel. 'They were astounded at his teaching,' he says of the people of Capernaum. 'That evening, at sunset, they brought to him all who were sick or possessed with demons. And the whole city was gathered round the door' (Mark 1.22a and 32–33). Capernaum was not a city but 'a modest village',[3] but we get the message. Jesus' fame spreads throughout Galilee like wildfire, 'so that,' Mark tells us, 'Jesus could no longer go into a town openly, but stayed out in the country; and people came to him from every quarter' (1.45b). That also is an exaggeration, for in the very next verse Jesus is back in Capernaum. But now, when four friends bring a paralysed man to him, they cannot even get near the door of his house and have to make a hole in the roof (2.2–4).

> Jesus went out again beside the lake [the sea of Galilee]; the whole crowd gathered around him, and he taught them . . . And as he sat at dinner in Levi's house, many tax-collectors and sinners were also sitting with Jesus and his disciples – for there were many who followed him.   (2.13, 15)

Mark's Greek in that second verse is somewhat ambiguous, but he appears to make a distinction between the 'disciples' and the rest of the people who are there. To be a disciple in Mark's eyes it is not enough to come to Jesus for wisdom or for healing. You have to join his new family and share in his work of establishing the kingdom of God. And you have to be prepared to bear the cost.

Back in chapter 1 there is a passage much celebrated by Christian preachers:

> As Jesus passed along the Sea of Galilee, he saw Simon and his brother Andrew casting a net into the lake – for they were fishermen. And Jesus said to them, 'Follow me and I will make you fish for people.' And immediately they left their nets and followed him. As he went a little farther, he saw James son of Zebedee and his brother John, who were in their boat mending the nets. Immediately he called them; and they left their father Zebedee in the boat with the hired men, and followed him.   (1.16–20)

In the next chapter we hear of his encounter with Levi son of Alphaeus: 'As he was walking along, he saw Levi son of Alphaeus sitting at the tax booth, and he said to him, "Follow me." And he got up and followed him' (2.14). Soon after that comes this:

> He went up the mountain and called to him those whom he wanted, and they came to him. And he appointed twelve, whom he also named apostles, to be with him, and to be sent out to proclaim the message, and to have authority to cast out demons. So he appointed the twelve: Simon (to whom he gave the name Peter); James son of Zebedee and John the brother of James . . . and Andrew, and Philip, and Bartholomew, and Matthew, and Thomas, and James son of Alphaeus, and Thaddaeus, and Simon the Cananaean, and Judas Iscariot, who betrayed him. (3.13–19)

These three passages and their parallels in Matthew and Luke are among the ones chiefly responsible for the belief that Jesus had as his disciples but 12 men, those and the stories of the Last Supper, where Mark and Matthew tell us Jesus ate the meal with 'the twelve' (Mark 14.17; Matthew 26.20), and Luke says he was with 'the apostles' (22.14). Then there are three verses in Matthew which speak of Jesus and 'his twelve disciples': 'Then Jesus summoned his twelve disciples' (Matthew 10.1); 'Now when Jesus had finished instructing his twelve disciples' (11.1); 'While Jesus was going up to Jerusalem, he took the twelve disciples aside' (20.17). The belief of that woman who led our prayers in my parish church can be readily understood.

In addition Mark, followed to an extent by Matthew and Luke, presents us with an inner circle of three, again all men. Jesus takes just Peter, James and his brother John inside the house of Jairus when he comes to raise his daughter from the dead (Mark 5.37; Luke 8.51; Matthew's account is much shorter and does not pick out the three men); they alone witness his Transfiguration (Mark 9.2; Matthew 17.1; Luke 9.28); he teaches them privately (Mark 13.3 – and only Mark); he takes them with him as his companions to share in his prayer and shaking distress in the Garden of Gethsemane (Mark 14.33; Matthew 26.37).

There has in the past been some debate among New Testament scholars about whether Jesus did indeed appoint 12 men to follow him, or whether 'the Twelve' was an invention of the early Church. The earliest reference to them is in fact not in the Gospels but in Paul's First Letter to the Corinthians, written some years before Mark, when he speaks of the tradition he had himself received, and talks of the risen Christ appearing first to Peter, then to 'the twelve' (see 1 Corinthians 15.3 and 5). That points to a very early date for 'the twelve', while the confusion about some of them in the Gospels and their obscurity point even more strongly to their originating with Jesus himself.

John makes reference to them but does not name them all, and it is not clear who he means to include. He has a story about the time when Andrew and Peter first meet Jesus, and immediately after that another about Jesus calling Philip to follow him (1.35–43). But instead of the call of James and John he tells of Philip bringing a Nathanael to Jesus (1.45–51). Nathanael is nowhere mentioned in the other Gospels. Does John mean to include him in 'the twelve'? That is not clear. He is not mentioned again until chapter 21, verse 2. There he is one of just seven disciples to meet the risen Jesus beside the Sea of Galilee, two of them left unnamed. Yet there remains some uncertainty about the authorship of that chapter, since John brings his Gospel to a formal conclusion at the end of chapter 20. Whether or not he composed chapter 21, he seems to be little interested in the Twelve as a body. Thomas is described as 'one of the twelve' in 20.24, but otherwise they are mentioned (three times) in only one other passage, 6.66–71.

In the other three Gospels their names do not quite match up. Instead of Thaddaeus in Mark and Matthew, Luke has Simon the Zealot, and, in place of their Simon the Cananean, Judas son of James. Furthermore, as all preachers know who have had the misfortune to preach on their festivals, almost half the Twelve are but names on a list. There are stories about Philip and Thomas in John (though only in John), and a very brief one about Matthew (Matthew 9.9), but we are given none at all about Bartholomew, James son of Alphaeus, Thaddaeus, Simon the Zealot, Simon the Cananean or Judas son of James – nor anything about that James or Alphaeus. Even stories of their call are missing. It seems the Twelve as a body, and those among them who are given no colour in their cheeks, played little or no significant role in the early Church, at least none that was remembered. That makes it very unlikely that their appointment was an invention of the Church after Jesus' death and resurrection.

Nor is it difficult to see why Jesus might have chosen them. The people of Israel had originally consisted of 12 tribes, named after the 12 sons of Jacob. Along with John the Baptist, Jesus believed it was time for Israel to go back to its roots. John drew people to the ancient border of the Promised Land, to the Jordan river, which they had once crossed with Joshua at the beginnings of their history as a nation. Baptism in the river's waters was John's symbolic act. Jesus' was the appointment of the Twelve. Had not Joshua himself selected 12 men, one from each of the tribes, as his first act after the safe crossing of the river (Joshua 4.1–7)? It is most certainly to be regretted that Jesus did not choose any women among them, but had he done so the symbolism would surely have been damaged or lost altogether.

Yet though Jesus' establishing the Twelve is probably authentic, it does not mean he went about with just those 12 men, or indeed that those 12 were closer to him than others. We have already examined, in our first chapter, the remarkable story of the woman who anoints Jesus' feet in Luke, and the one about the woman who anoints his head in Mark and Matthew. In each case, when we set her tale against the larger narratives of those Gospels, we see that her devotion to Jesus, her love for him, as well as her wisdom and understanding, put the Twelve and the other male disciples to shame.

We must continue, however, to clear the ground before we can turn to other stories of Jesus' women followers and hope to do them justice.

What do the Evangelists mean by 'the disciples'?

In that last section we quoted three verses from Matthew that spoke of Jesus and 'his twelve disciples'. Yet Matthew also has this: 'Another of his disciples said to him, "Lord, first let me go and bury my father." But Jesus said to him, "Follow me, and let the dead bury their own dead" '(8.21–22). It is clear enough that this 'disciple' is not among the Twelve. Looking at the use of the word 'disciple' in all four Gospels, Pierson Parker writes:

> Of over two hundred and thirty instances of the term in the gospels, about ninety per cent either are not limited to the Twelve at all, or else do not make clear whether these or some larger group is indicated.[4]

In all those 230 occurrences, however, we find no explicit reference to women. Only once in the whole of the New Testament do we come across a woman who is called a disciple, Tabitha in Acts 9.36, but by then the term has become synonymous with 'Christian'. In the Gospel passages concerning 'the disciples', when particular individuals are named or referred to, they are always men.

There are no stories in any of the Gospels about Jesus calling a woman to follow him. In addition to the small number of call stories already quoted, there is John 1.43, where he says to Philip, 'Follow me', and the story of the 'rich man' in Mark, the one Matthew describes simply as a 'young man' and Luke as 'a certain ruler': in all three versions of that the man is challenged by Jesus to sell all he has, give the proceeds to the poor and then follow him (Mark 10.21; Matthew 19.21; Luke 18.22). Luke has his own version of the dialogue between Jesus and the one who asks to go and bury his father: Jesus again says to him, 'Follow me,' though this time he is not identified as a disciple (9.59–60).

There is a very interesting passage early on in Mark's Gospel which talks of Jesus teaching a crowd of people:

> Then his mother and his brothers came; and standing outside, they sent to him and called him. A crowd was sitting around him; and they said to him, 'Your mother and your brothers[5] are outside, asking for you.' And he replied, 'Who are my mother and my brothers?' And looking at those who sat around him, he said, 'Here are my mother and my brothers! Whoever does the will of God is my brother and sister and mother.' (Mark 3.31–35)

Elizabeth Fiorenza comments, '[T]hose who "do the will of God" come together in discipleship to form a new "household" '.

[W]omen are clearly included among the followers of Jesus . . . Whereas the narrative context stresses twice . . . that 'Jesus' mother and brother were outside calling him', the saying of Jesus refers to brothers, mother, and sisters.[6]

She is surely correct in what she says, and in the emphasis she lays upon Mark's reference to 'sisters'. Yet he does not describe them explicitly as coming together 'in discipleship', nor does he call them disciples, and elsewhere he would suggest that when he speaks of 'the disciples' he is thinking only of men. He begins his story of Jesus praying in Gethsemane by telling us, 'They went to a place called Gethsemane; and he said to *his disciples*, "Sit here while I pray" ' (14.32). Towards the end of the following story of Jesus' arrest he writes, '*All of them* deserted him and fled' (14.50). Yet when he comes to the crucifixion, he speaks of women looking on from a distance, who have followed Jesus from Galilee. (15.40) *They* have not deserted him and fled. So are they not disciples? Surely they are, and they would appear at this point to be his most devoted and courageous ones. But Mark does not appear to think of them as such. We might point out that in the Gethsemane story 'the disciples' is but another way of speaking of the Twelve, as the preceding passage about the Last Supper makes clear (see Mark 14.12 and 17). Yet that does not let Mark off the hook. He could have easily written in 15.40, 'There were also *some women disciples* looking on from a distance'. It is a matter of Mark's use of language and the mind-set that is driving it.

The other Gospels tell a similar tale. Matthew concludes his version of the arrest with the words, 'Then *all the disciples* deserted him and fled' (26.56b), only to tell us when he reaches the cross, 'Many women were also there . . . they had followed Jesus from Galilee' (27.55). Luke speaks of 'the women who had come with him from Galilee' witnessing Jesus' burial (23.55), then going to his tomb to find it full of heaven. They rush back to report their encounter 'to the eleven' (Judas Iscariot has left the Twelve in betraying Jesus) '*and to all the rest*' (24.9). We know the women do not belong to the Twelve; they seem not to belong to 'the rest' either. John gives a broad definition of the disciples in the course of his earlier narrative when he has Jesus say, 'If you continue in my word, you are truly my disciples;

39

and you will know the truth, and the truth will make you free' (8.31–32). In these words, however, he is clearly addressing the people of his own day, those listening to his Gospel being performed. When his mind is on those 'disciples' who accompanied Jesus during his ministry, he appears to exclude women from their company in the same way as the other Evangelists. At the end of his story of Mary of Magdala meeting the risen Jesus he tells us she 'went and announced to the disciples, "I have seen the Lord" ' (20.18). He could have said she 'announced to the *other* disciples', or 'to *her fellow* disciples', but he does not – despite the fact that he has just told a story that marks Mary out as more steadfast in her devotion to Jesus and to the truth than either Peter or the one called 'the beloved disciple'.

In conclusion, therefore, when any of the Evangelists talk of 'the disciples', though they may not always mean just the Twelve, they do not seem to be thinking of the women among them, but only of the men.

The failure of the men

Mark is notorious for his negative portrayal of 'the disciples', even of the three who form Jesus' inner circle. But Mark is not the only one, as we shall see.

Mark, Matthew and Luke punctuate their narratives with predictions of Jesus' Passion. Their Gospels (and John's also, of course) slowly build up to the climax of Jesus' arrest, crucifixion and resurrection, and Jesus tries to prepare the disciples for what is to come. In Mark the first occasion goes like this:

> Jesus went on with his disciples to the villages of Caesarea Philippi; and on the way he asked his disciples, 'Who do people say that I am?' And they answered, 'John the Baptist; and others, Elijah; and still others, one of the prophets.' He asked them, 'But who do you say that I am?' Peter answered him, 'You are the Messiah.' And he sternly ordered them not to tell anyone about him. Then he began to teach them that the Son of Man must undergo great suffering, and be rejected by the elders, the chief priests, and the scribes, and be killed, and after three days rise again. He said all this quite openly. And Peter took him aside and began to rebuke him. But turning and looking at his disciples, he rebuked Peter and said, 'Get behind me, Satan! For you are setting your mind not on divine things but on human things.' He called the crowd with his disciples, and said to them, 'If any want to become my followers, let them deny themselves and take up their cross and follow me. For those who want to save their life will lose it, and those who lose their life for my sake, and for the sake of the gospel, will save it.' (8.27–35)

Peter has come in for high praise for his insight into Jesus' being the Messiah. After all, in Mark's Greek 'You are the Messiah' appears as 'You are the Christ.' It is the first time in Mark that anyone has called Jesus that. In Matthew's telling of the story, Peter is praised by Jesus himself, and extravagantly so.

> Blessed are you, Simon son of Jonah! For flesh and blood has not revealed this to you, but my Father in heaven. And I tell you, you are Peter, and on this rock I will build my church . . . I will give you the keys of the kingdom of heaven. (Matthew 16.17–19a)

Jesus' response in Mark, however, is more ambiguous, and it is not even clear whether he is accepting the title Messiah from Peter, or not. The ambiguity is more marked in the Greek, where we find the word behind the phrase: '*he sternly ordered* them' is the same as the one used twice a little later in the passage and there translated 'rebuke' or 'rebuked'. But there is no doubt about what Nineham rightly calls 'the blistering severity'[7] of Jesus' reply to Peter, 'Get behind me, Satan!', words which are repeated exactly by Matthew in his version (16.23). 'Get behind me!' probably means, 'Get out of my sight!'[8] and that is devastating enough, but it is the 'Satan!' which is truly shocking. Luke and John will tell us that 'Satan entered into' Judas Iscariot and drove him to betray Jesus to the authorities (Luke 22.3; John 13.27), but no one else in the Gospels is called Satan, except for Satan himself in Matthew's version of the temptations in the wilderness, where Jesus says, 'Away with you, Satan!' (Matthew 4.10). In the Greek text 'Away with you!' is much closer to 'Get behind me!' than we might suppose: the same verb is used in each phrase. The echo in the Greek is unmistakable. Mark's version of the temptations in the wilderness is much briefer than Matthew's and contains no dialogue (1.12–13). He waits till chapter 8 to make plain what those earlier temptations amounted to: setting one's mind not on divine things but on human things; trying to do the work of God without any suffering. As Jesus explains in 8.31 and 34, he *must* undergo great suffering, and those who follow him must be prepared to take up their own cross – a truly terrifying way of describing the cost of discipleship. These verses bracket Peter's protestation and Jesus' rebuking him. And so they do in Matthew, whose version is very similar to Mark's.

Luke is kinder to Peter. Though he includes Peter's confession, Jesus' prediction of his death and the teaching about taking up one's cross, he omits the dialogue which is so damaging. In Luke Peter does not rebuke Jesus; Jesus does not rebuke him in return (see Luke 9.18–24). Of the three versions, Matthew's is the most striking, for he is the one who raises Peter to such heights – nowhere else is Peter declared the rock on which the Church will be built; nowhere else is he given the keys of heaven – only to bring him tumbling down to the very depths a very few verses later.

If Luke here lets Peter off the hook, he is not so lenient with the disciples elsewhere, as we will soon discover.

Mark 8.31 is the first time in that Gospel that Jesus speaks to his disciples of his death; 9.31 is the second. Its language is similar to the first, and Mark comments, 'But they did not understand what he was saying and were afraid to ask' (9.32). Peter dare not intervene a second time, and the others share his caution and his fear of rebuke. But then Mark proceeds immediately with this:

> Then they came to Capernaum; and when he was in the house he asked them, 'What were you arguing about on the way?' But they were silent, for on the way they had argued with one another about who was the greatest. He sat down, called the twelve, and said to them, 'Whoever wants to be first must be last of all and servant of all.' Then he took a little child and put it among them; and taking it in his arms, he said to them, 'Whoever welcomes one such child in my name welcomes me, and whoever welcomes me welcomes not me but the one who sent me.'   (9.33–37)

Mark's Gospel is a work of genius. If we think he has simply strung unconnected episodes together, then we do not recognize his artistry. It is no accident that he has followed Jesus' second prediction of his death by the disciples arguing among themselves, and done so without a break. He has thereby made their arguing immeasurably more shocking. No wonder they are covered in shame and fall into silence. Has the Jesus they are following in this Gospel ever tried to put himself forward as 'the greatest'? No, he has not. From the beginning he has set his mind firmly on divine things, not on human things, and not long ago he has spoken of his followers needing to 'deny themselves and take up their cross'. In between the two predictions of Jesus' death Mark places the story of the Transfiguration (9.2–8). In that story Jesus takes Peter, James and John with him up his new Mount Sinai, and there the veil is lifted and he is revealed shining with all the ancient glory of God. Come their return to Capernaum, therefore, Peter, James and John have just gone deep into the very mystery of God; they have in effect gone inside the Holy of Holies; they have seen and heard God. Yet here they are joining in the arguments about which one of their number is the greatest!

If we protest they are not mentioned by name – though notice Mark does not exclude them, either – then wait just another chapter for Jesus' third prediction of his death. Mark goes into more detail this time: speaks of Jesus being handed over to the Romans for execution, of their mockery, their covering him with their spittle, their flogging him . . . and then their killing him. The language could not be plainer. Yet Mark follows it with this, without a blink in between:

> James and John, the sons of Zebedee, came forward to him and said to him, 'Teacher, we want you to do for us whatever we ask of you.' And

he said to them, 'What is it you want me to do for you?' And they said
to him, *'Grant us to sit, one at your right hand and one at your left, in
your glory.'*   (10.35–37)

James and John, remember, are, like Peter, members of Jesus' innermost circle – or so Mark has presented them. It is as if they understand nothing. It is as if Jesus has never opened his mouth; as if the
Transfiguration has counted for nothing; as if the crossing of the sea
and the healing of the man among the tombs and all the rest has
never happened.

And so it is with Mark's other 'disciples'. Between the second and
third predictions of Jesus' death he includes a short piece about people bringing small children to Jesus, in order that he might touch
them and heal them. He continues: 'and the disciples spoke sternly
to them' (there's that same verb again, the one that can be translated
'rebuked').

> But when Jesus saw this, he was indignant and said to them, 'Let
> the little children come to me; do not stop them; for it is to such
> as these that the kingdom of God belongs. Truly I tell you, whoever
> does not receive the kingdom of God as a little child will never enter
> it.' And he took them up in his arms, laid his hands on them, and
> blessed them.   (10.13–16)

Has not Jesus just before this taken a little child in his arms, expressly
in order to teach the disciples about the kingdom of God? Has he not
just said, 'Whoever welcomes one such child in my name welcomes
me, and whoever welcomes me welcomes not me but the one who
sent me?' By that token, when the disciples try to turn the little children away, they are turning Jesus away, they are turning *God* away.

It is a sorry tale, and all these passages have their parallels in both
Matthew and Luke. Matthew softens the impact of the disciples arguing among themselves considerably. He follows Jesus' second prediction of his Passion with a passage about the Temple tax, and then
he has the disciples not arguing among themselves but asking Jesus,
'Who is the greatest in the kingdom of heaven?' (Matthew 18.1) And
when it comes to Jesus' third prediction, he has the *mother* of James
and John kneeling before him and asking, 'Declare that these two
sons of mine will sit, one at your right hand and one at your left,
in your kingdom' (20.20–21). But in this case Matthew's stratagem
is far from convincing, and it is as if he does not really believe in it

himself. For Jesus addresses his reply not to the mother but to the disciples (Greek grammar distinguishes between 'you' singular and 'you' plural, and each 'you' in 20.22–23 is in the plural form), and he enters into dialogue with them, not with her; the other ten disciples are then described as being angry with the two brothers, rather than their mother (20.24).

Before we leave Matthew, however, we should recall that in his version of the woman who anoints Jesus' head it is he who speaks of the anger of 'the disciples' (26.8), whereas Mark is more vague, talking only of 'some who were there' (14.4). In that case – and what a significant one it is! – it is Matthew who intensifies Mark's criticism of the disciples. And he does so further by the way he handles the context of the anointing, for he prefaces that story with another occasion when Jesus speaks to his disciples of his death (Matthew 26.1–2). Mark, at that point, simply reports that the chief priests and scribes were looking for a way to arrest him (Mark 14.1–2).

Though Luke omits Peter's protest and Jesus' rebuke when first Jesus speaks of his Passion, he comments, when he comes to the second prediction, 'But they did not understand this saying; its meaning was concealed from them, so that they could not perceive it. And they were afraid to ask him about this saying' (Luke 9.45). And then he follows Mark, not Matthew, by launching straight into, 'An argument arose among them as to which one of them was the greatest' (9.46). He also includes (as does Matthew) Jesus' lesson of the little child, and then later the story of the disciples trying to stop the little children reaching him (Luke 9.47–48, 18.15; Matthew 18.2–5, 19.13). And though he does not speak of James and John, or their mother, asking for the best places in Jesus' kingdom, he does include this story, unique to his Gospel:

> [Jesus] set his face to go to Jerusalem. And he sent messengers ahead of him. On their way they entered a village of the Samaritans to make ready for him; but they did not receive him, because his face was set towards Jerusalem. When his disciples James and John saw it, they said, 'Lord, do you want us to command fire to come down from heaven and consume them?' But he turned and rebuked them.   (Luke 9.51b–55)

There's that word 'rebuke' again (the same verb in the Greek as before). Well might Luke use it, for as we see from the chapter and verse reference, this passage comes almost immediately after James and John have heard Jesus speaking of his betrayal and seen him with the little child. What, we might ask, are they thinking of?

And having repeated that the disciples could not begin to understand Jesus when he spoke of his death, or grasp what was being said (18.34), Luke includes a *second* passage where they dispute among themselves which one of them is to be regarded as the greatest (it begins at 22.24). He too underscores how shocking such argument is by carefully placing it at a particular point in his narrative: in the course of the Last Supper, no less, and just after Judas Iscariot has left to confer with the chief priests and officers of the Temple police about the betrayal. *Have they still learned nothing?*

It is not just Mark. In Matthew and Luke also the male disciples, the Twelve, and the three presented as closest to Jesus, all come in for fearful criticism. Furthermore, as everyone knows and as all four Gospels assert, Judas Iscariot, one of the Twelve, betrays him, and Peter denies he knows him. And in Mark and Matthew certainly (Luke's text has a measure of ambiguity), none of the male disciples will be there at the cross, or at Jesus' burial. *They* do not take up their cross to follow Jesus. 'All of them deserted him and fled,' says Mark (14.50) and Matthew says the same (26.56). It is not surprising that they are not the first to stumble upon the resurrection. It is not surprising, either, though it is deeply shocking, that when in Luke Mary of Magdala, Joanna, Mary the mother of James and the other women return in high excitement from the empty tomb, the male disciples dismiss their reports as an idle tale (24.11), as the kind of thing hysterical females would say, wouldn't they, as if God does not communicate reliably with women – and this in a Gospel that begins with the annunciation to Mary of Nazareth![9]

So at last in this chapter we have reached the women! The rest of it will be devoted to them.

The women as witnesses of the crucifixion

'Follow me.' As we have seen, the list of those called by Jesus in the Gospels to follow him is short, and no women appear in it. But it cannot be complete. There are no call stories for six members of the Twelve. He 'appoints' (Mark 3.14) or 'chooses' (Luke 6.13) the Twelve as a body, but surely he must have called each of them individually. So when we hear of women following him, we should not presume he did not invite each of them to join the family of his disciples and accompany him on the road. Because, as we have already glimpsed from the crucifixion narratives, some women did follow him, and we know their names, or the names of some of them at least.

We have already wondered whether we should think of the woman who anoints Jesus in Luke as being a follower and disciple of his, and we posed the same question, even more forcefully, of the woman who anoints him in Mark and Matthew. But we do not always have to rely on hints and veiled implications. Let us quote in full the two verses in Mark which speak of the women present at the crucifixion:

> There were also women looking on from a distance; among them were Mary Magdalene, and Mary the mother of James the younger and of Joses, and Salome. These used to follow him and provided for him when he was in Galilee; and there were many other women who had come up with him to Jerusalem. (Mark 15.40–41)

So now we know.

This is the first time Mark has even mentioned these women. But they have been there all the time, at least for a goodly portion of it, hidden in the shadows of the narrative. Is it because they are women that they have hitherto remained invisible? The question has to be asked, but it cannot be answered with certainty. At the beginning of Acts Luke has Peter raise the issue of the missing member of the Twelve. Judas Iscariot has left their number and has since died. Peter addresses 'the believers' in these words:

> So one of the men who have accompanied us during all the time that the Lord Jesus went in and out among us, beginning from the baptism of John until the day when he was taken up from us – one of these must become a witness with us to his resurrection.

So they proposed,' Luke continues, 'two, Joseph called Barsabbas, who was also known as Justus, and Matthias' (Acts 1.21–23). Luke makes no reference to either of these men in the course of his Gospel (and they do not feature in any of the other Gospels either). Yet it seems they have been followers of Jesus for his entire ministry. They, too, have been completely invisible.

In Mark, to give another example, just before Jesus enters Jerusalem on his borrowed colt, he encounters a blind man called Bartimaeus as he is leaving Jericho. Bartimaeus calls for Jesus to have mercy on him, and Jesus stops and addresses him. Mark's story proceeds with this: ' "What do you want me to do for you?" The blind man said to him, "My teacher, let me see again." Jesus said to him, "Go; your faith has made you well." ' The story then closes with, 'Immediately he regained his sight and followed him on the way' (10.51–52). 'He followed him on the way.' That is particularly intriguing, for Jesus is travelling to Jerusalem and to the death he has predicted. So do we find reference to Bartimaeus in Mark's Passion narrative? No. Should we imagine he too deserts Jesus and flees with the other male disciples? Or should we picture him there at the cross with the women? We cannot say. He is a typical one-scener. He has his story and then is gone.

Yet Mark's complete silence about the women until he gets to 15.40–41 remains especially unnerving, for they are there *at the crucifixion*. Yes, they are 'at a distance', here and in Matthew 27.55 and Luke 23.49 also, but we should be careful what we make of that. Joel Green, commenting on Luke 23.49, cites Psalm 38.11,

> My friends and companions stand aloof from my affliction,
> and my neighbours stand far off

and then says of those standing at a distance from the cross, 'their geographical remoteness indicates a weakened discipleship that is as yet unwilling to identify too closely with Jesus in his humiliation and death'.[10] Warren Carter's judgement on the women in Matthew 27.55, is quite different:

> Unlike the male disciples, they have not fled (26.56). The phrase 'from the distance' links them with Peter, who also follows Jesus 'from a distance' to the courtyard in 26.58. But whereas he denies Jesus and departs, the women remain faithful in walking the way of the cross (16.24–26).[11]

The truth of it may have been rather more mundane. The Roman soldiers in charge of the crucifixion may very well have not allowed the women to come any closer, or else they knew they had to avoid being identified by those same soldiers as followers of a man whom Pilate had condemned as a danger to the state. As witnesses of Jesus' death the women told their fellow disciples that they had had to stand at a distance, and it was their honesty that formed the tradition. Whatever the case, Green's description of their 'weakened discipleship' is unreasonably harsh.

And however we interpret their being 'at a distance', the women are there, witnessing what all the Gospels agree is the most significant moment of all, that and the resurrection. And they are there, too, at least in the mysterious territory of its aftermath.

Surely Mark, to focus again on his version, might have told us of these women before. They are not really one-sceners, after all. They have been following Jesus within Galilee and on his journey towards Jerusalem. Jesus and the rest of his new family have depended on them for their financial support. They have helped make his mission possible.

In his account of the crucifixion John places a single unnamed male disciple at the cross among a small group of women, the man described throughout that Gospel as 'the one Jesus loved' (19.25–26). And Luke, who quite often has more extras in his scenes than the others, says somewhat vaguely, 'But all his acquaintances, including the women who had followed him from Galilee, stood at a distance, watching these things' (23.49). Given what we learn from the other Gospels, his reference to 'all his acquaintances' is not entirely convincing, but even he makes special mention of the women. In Mark and Matthew the women are there on their own.

The women and the resurrection

Matthew describes how Mary of Magdala and Mary the mother of James and Joseph are the first to meet the risen Jesus. The angel at the tomb tells them that Jesus is going ahead of them to Galilee, and that they and the other disciples will see him there (28.7). But as they run off to tell the others, Jesus suddenly greets them (28.9–10). The encounter is quite unexpected. In John, Mary of Magdala is on her own when the risen Jesus appears (20.11). She is the first to see him.

Perhaps through no fault of his own Mark leaves things unclear. In his story of the empty tomb his Gospel ends abruptly with the angel telling the women, 'Go, tell his disciples and Peter that he is going ahead of you to Galilee; there you will see him, just as he told you'; and then, 'So they went out and fled from the tomb, for terror and amazement had seized them; and they said nothing to anyone, for they were afraid' (16.7–8). For some considerable time scholars have hailed this as a master-stroke. It is not. The story of Jesus could not end, did not end with people running away and keeping their mouths shut for very fear. It can only end, it *did* end with people encountering the risen Jesus, and in the falling of everything into place, the place of God's merriment, hope and love. Mark himself predicts such an encounter in his penultimate verse, a prediction which is repeating what Jesus himself has said in 14.28, 'After I am raised up, I will go before you to Galilee.' Mark is not in the habit of making predictions and then not reporting their fulfilment. That has been pointed out by Clayton Croy.[12] Croy devotes a whole book to arguing that the original ending (and the beginning) of Mark's Gospel were lost when the codex or book containing it was taken round the Christian communities, and N. T. Wright supports his theory of a missing ending.[13] Let us imagine ourselves for a moment being among those Christians who first heard Mark's Gospel read. Mark did not envisage that his great story would be read by individuals in their book-lined studies. His work was designed to be performed live to Christian communities. Many Christians in those days could not read, not because they were especially poor but because most people then could not read. And they all belonged, whether literate or not, to an oral culture, where the spoken word was the main means of communication. They would have heard many performances of the story of Jesus before, and they knew it began with John the Baptist and ended with Jesus appearing to his disciples soon after his death, wrapped in the light of resurrection and the glory of God. When they first heard Mark, had his story ended with the women running away from the tomb they would surely have protested, 'But you can't end there! You've omitted the climax of it all! You've left out the very stories that explain why we're here! You *can't* end there!' In our view, despite the fact that a large scholarly consensus is against them, Croy and Wright are correct: Mark's original ending is lost. Whether he went straight on to speak of Jesus appearing to his disciples, including the women, in Galilee, or whether, like Matthew, he surprised his hearers by telling of Jesus meeting the women on the way, we will never know. Whatever the case, he knew full well that the women had *not* kept their mouths shut, not once they reached the others. For otherwise how could the story of their vision at the tomb have got out?

John has the beloved disciple at the cross for a very particular reason. He makes the moment immediately before Jesus dies the occasion of the founding of the Church. That is conceived, not as a great public institution, but as a new household, and for the formation of a new household you need, in John's world, a man and a woman. For that reason the beloved disciple must be there, and so too, remarkably, Jesus' own mother, and they must both stand, not at a distance, but at the very foot of the cross, for they need to hear what Jesus has to say to them. John's words are charged with almost unbearable poignancy and compassion – and with hope: 'When Jesus saw his mother and the disciple whom he loved standing beside her, he said to his mother, "Woman, here is your son." Then he said to the disciple, "Here is your mother" ' (19.26–27). Three others are there, and they are all women, 'his mother's sister, Mary the wife of Clopas, and Mary Magdalene' (19.25), and the third of those will be the first to meet the risen Jesus. Her story in John 20, where she stands weeping outside the tomb and hears the risen Jesus call her name, is the finest of the resurrection stories in any of the Gospels by a country mile, and goes some way to explain why, when the other Evangelists speak of the women at the cross and at the tomb, they always put Mary of Magdala at the head of the list.

With another woman or women, whose presence in the narrative is given away by the plural form of a single verb in John 20.2, Mary discovers Jesus' tomb to be empty, and runs back to tell the others. We might suppose that all of them will then go rushing off to the tomb, but only Peter and the beloved disciple do so. There Peter finds mere absence, an emptiness and his own bewilderment. The beloved disciple realizes the truth; inside the tomb, so John tells us, he sees and believes. Yet then the two men go away; they return to their homes. Only Mary remains. 'But Mary stood weeping outside the tomb' (20.11). We do not have the space to examine in detail her meeting with the risen Jesus that John decribes.[14] Suffice to say it appears from John's narrative that her grief is sharper than that of Peter and the other disciple, and her devotion to Jesus stronger than theirs. She has been completely invisible in John's story prior to the crucifixion, and now she emerges as perhaps Jesus' closest disciple.

Luke plays down the part played by the women. The first to meet the risen Jesus are not the women at the tomb, but a Cleopas and his companion (his wife?) we have never heard of before (the famous story of the Walk to Emmaus in 24.13–35) and Simon Peter. Rather curiously, Luke tells no story of the appearance to Peter. Cleopas and his companion return to Jerusalem to find 'the eleven and their companions', saying, 'The Lord has risen indeed, and he has appeared to Simon!' (Luke 24.33, 34). That is all. Though the tradition of Peter being the first to encounter the risen Jesus is very early, and is reported by Paul in 1 Corinthians 15.5, nevertheless, if we take all the Gospels together, we are drawn to conclude it was the women disciples who first told the stories of Jesus' crucifixion, burial and resurrection, for the simple reason they were there. They witnessed those events, or at least, in the case of the resurrection, came hard on its heels. The male disciples did not, though they subsequently had their own encounters with the risen Jesus. We cannot trust Luke's reference to 'all Jesus' acquaintances' at the cross, and his resurrection stories (as well as Paul's report in 1 Corinthians 15.5) may reflect disquiet in some circles in the early Church that the truth of the resurrection should first have been discovered by women. Certainly, when he comes to write Acts, the second volume of his great masterpiece, Luke fills the pages with Peter and Paul, and the women disciples who appear in the Gospels are written out, except for a single, tantalizing reference to 'certain women' and Mary, Jesus' mother, in Acts 1.14.

It is highly unlikely that the early Church invented the tradition of the part played by some women in these events. For whether or not we have interpreted Luke's treatment of the resurrection aright, the stories of the women would have caused considerable embarrassment in some circles within the Church, and would have made it harder for those outside to accept a proclamation that was already, in the memorable words of Paul, 'a stumbling-block to Jews and foolishness to Gentiles' (1 Corinthians 1.23). Indeed, Luke's story about the male disciples dismissing the reports of the women about the empty tomb as 'an idle tale' (24.11) is evidence that such embarrassment *was* caused, and that their stories could sometimes meet with scorn.

Joanna and the disconsolate rich man

The women at the cross in Mark appear out of the blue. So do Mary of Magdala in John and her companions at the cross, Jesus' aunt and Mary the wife of Clopas. Matthew tells of the mother of James and John being there (27.56), and as we have seen, he has introduced us to her before, in 20.20, when she asks Jesus to secure positions of power in his kingdom for her sons. Although Matthew's handling of her part in that episode is clumsy and unconvincing, nevertheless it does remind us that the disciples did include women. There was no mention of her when her sons were called away from their boat on the Sea of Galilee, and yet it seems she too became a disciple, and when it came to the crunch and Jesus was executed, she did not, like her two sons, desert him and flee. Matthew gives the name of her husband, Zebedee, though he tells us he did not become a follower (James and John leave him behind in 4.21) and does not mention him at the cross. She herself, alas, is left unnamed.

In John Mary, Jesus' mother, appears in chapter 2 and plays an important part in the story of the wedding at Cana. Apart from that story and the one in Matthew 20, there is only one other place in the Gospels where any of the women who are named in the crucifixion scenes appear in the narrative beforehand. The passage concerned has been quoted already in the last chapter, with reference to the woman who anoints Jesus in Luke 7. We need to quote it again. It is short, but it tells us a good deal.

> Soon afterwards he went on through cities and villages, proclaiming and bringing the good news of the kingdom of God. The twelve were with him, as well as some women who had been cured of evil spirits and infirmities: Mary, called Magdalene, from whom seven demons had gone out, and Joanna, the wife of Herod's steward Chuza, and Susanna, and many others, who provided for them out of their resources.
> (Luke 8.1–3; the 'many others' is feminine in the Greek text, and so indicates many other women)

Joanna's presence at the cross is implied by Luke, when he speaks there of 'the women who had followed him from Galilee', and she is mentioned by name among the women who find the empty tomb. That is all we have, but the naming of her husband Chuza, and the description of him being Herod's steward, is exceptional and mighty interesting. It would suggest Joanna was one of the main contributors to the common fund on which Jesus and his other disciples drew. But it suggests much more than that.

I have been a Christian all my life and am now in my 70s. In all that time I have never heard a sermon preached on Joanna, except for two I preached myself.[15] Of course I might have missed a great many, but the fact remains that while I have heard countless sermons on the call and discipleship of Peter and Andrew, James and John, many even on Judas Iscariot, I have heard just two, my own, on Joanna. I know of no church dedicated to her. She has a role in two films made in 2015 for American television, *Killing Jesus* and *AD: The Bible Continues*, yet few commentators have done her justice. A shining exception is Richard Bauckham, who devotes 94 pages of painstaking scholarship to her in his book *Gospel Women*.[16]

Bauckham explains the significance of Joanna's social position. The Herod referred to by Luke is not the Herod of Matthew's story of the magi, but his son Herod Antipas, tetrarch or ruler of Galilee. Luke does not give him a good press. He is the one responsible for the death of John the Baptist, and though Luke does not include any story of the events leading up to that death such as we find in Mark 6.14–29 and Matthew 14.1–12, he does make reference in 9.9 to Herod's having beheaded him. In Luke 13.31 we hear of some Pharisees, sympathetic to Jesus and his cause, who warn him to 'Get away from here, for Herod wants to kill you.' Only Luke tells us that, and only Luke, in the course of his Passion narrative, has Pilate send Jesus to Herod when he learns he is 'under Herod's jurisdiction' (23.7). That passage ends with the words, 'Herod with his soldiers treated him with contempt and mocked him; then he put an elegant robe on him, and sent him back to Pilate. That same day Herod and Pilate became friends' (23.11–12a). It is from the court of this same Herod in Tiberias that Joanna comes. And her husband Chuza is a high-ranking official there.

The term Luke uses to describe Chuza is ambiguous, but Bauckham discusses it at some length and suggests it could mean he was Herod's finance minister, in charge of his property and revenues.[17] Early in his reign Herod built three new cities in Galilee, Sepphoris, Livias and Tiberias itself. Large sums of money would have been needed for these projects, no doubt raised through taxation, which would not have endeared Herod or the likes of Chuza to the people in the Galilean villages. Bauckham describes the places as 'the first real cities built in Galilee', and says of Sepphoris and Tiberias that they must have 'seemed a culturally alien intrusion into Galilee, "aggressive acts of Romanization by Antipas," as Sean Freyne calls them'.[18] To make matters worse for Tiberias, it was built on the site of a cemetery, which would have further offended religious Jews, and Galilee was a very religious place. By the time Jesus began his ministry, Tiberias had only been standing for ten years and feelings would still have been raw.

This is the world from which Joanna comes, a world denounced, according to Luke, by Jesus himself. For in Luke 7.24–26 he speaks to the crowds about John the Baptist. 'What did you go out into the wilderness to look at?' he asks them.

> A reed shaken by the wind? What then did you go out to see? Someone dressed in soft robes? Look, those who put on fine clothing and live in luxury are in royal palaces. What then did you go out to see? A prophet? Yes, I tell you, and more than a prophet.

For royal palaces here think Tiberias, says Bauckham: 'for Jesus' Galilean hearers there was only one royal court worth mentioning and . . . it was Herod who had put John in prison'.[19] Joanna crosses what Bauckham rightly describes as a 'vast social gulf' when she joins Jesus and his entourage to become his follower and disciple.[20]

In all the Gospels it is in Luke that we find the greatest emphasis on Jesus' mission to the poor and oppressed. Right at the start of his ministry, in the synagogue in his home village of Nazareth, Jesus reads from the scroll of the prophet Isaiah:

> The Spirit of the Lord is upon me,
> because he has anointed me
> to bring good news to the poor.
> He has sent me to proclaim release to the captives
> and recovery of sight to the blind,
> to let the oppressed go free,
> to proclaim the year of the Lord's favour.
>
> (Luke 4.18–19)

Luke follows that with many a story of Jesus reaching out to those on or beyond the margins of society. Within his own circle he condemns any preoccupation with status, as we have already seen. More radically still, he pronounces a *reversal* of status in the kingdom of God: 'some are last who will be first, and some are first who will be last'

(Luke 13.30, with parallels in Mark and Matthew). In his version of another passage from Mark and Matthew, Luke has Jesus say to the 'apostles' at the Last Supper:

> The kings of the Gentiles lord it over them; and those in authority over them are called benefactors. But not so with you; rather the greatest among you must become like the youngest, and the leader like one who serves. For who is greater, the one who is at the table or the one who serves? Is it not the one at the table? But I am among you as one who serves. (22.25–27)

Jesus will never walk the corridors of power, or rather he will, but only as an arrested, mocked and beaten criminal, on his way to a form of execution carefully designed to parade him as an outcast, a piece of Pilate's and Herod's trash thrown out into what they suppose will be enduring oblivion. Bauckham deserves to be quoted at some length here:

> Joanna took the step of discipleship, for her a step across the whole social gulf that separated the Tiberian elite from the ordinary people, not to mention the beggars, the prostitutes, and other outcasts with whom Jesus habitually associated . . . Throwing in her lot with Jesus was a radical conversion to the poor, but it must have been the non-discriminating acceptance with which the community of Jesus' disciples welcomed all who joined them, even tax collectors, that gave her the confidence to risk her reputation among her peers, burning her bridges behind her, in order to identify herself as fully as possible with Jesus and his movement. Among these people, her status brought her no honour; not even her substantial donations to the common fund gave her a place above others. But instead she found a place in what Jesus called his new family of those who were practising the will of God, his sisters and brothers and mothers, who were therefore also sisters and brothers and mothers to each other.[21]

There is a story in Mark, Matthew and Luke, to which we have already made reference, of a rich man, a devout Jew, who approaches Jesus to ask him what he must do to inherit eternal life. It is found in Mark 10.17–22, Matthew 19.16–22 and Luke 18.18–25. Alone of the three Luke calls him a 'ruler' and so puts him within touching distance of Chuza's and Joanna's world. In answer to his question Jesus talks of obeying the Ten Commandments, and then, when the man tells him he has kept all of them since his youth, says to him, 'There is still one thing lacking. Sell all that you own and distribute the money to the poor, and you will have treasure in heaven; then come, follow me.' Luke continues,

> But when he heard this, he became sad; for he was very rich. Jesus looked at him and said, 'How hard it is for those who have wealth to enter the kingdom of God! Indeed, it is easier for a camel to go through the eye of a needle than for someone who is rich to enter the kingdom of God.'

That is a famous story, and has helped give rise to the widely held notion that all Jesus' followers were poor. But Joanna was not. She could not quite be described as a ruler, but Chuza could be, and Joanna herself had control over her own financial resources and would have been used to having considerable authority. *In her case the camel did go through the eye of the needle.* She was rich, probably very rich, but she did enter the kingdom of God and found home there. She did not sell all she had, and almost certainly Jesus did not ask her to. But she no longer used her wealth for her own comfort and aggrandisement. Instead she used it for the benefit of her new family and the man at its centre who had healed her (see Luke 8.2), who had so inspired her and who had turned her life upside down. It is right, of course, that Peter and Andrew, James and John receive our admiration and our praise for leaving everything to follow Jesus. But what about Joanna? Her sacrifice was greater than theirs and more remarkable. Indeed, it was astonishing. The court of Herod Antipas is surely among the last places we would have expected a follower of Jesus to have come from.

The story of the disconsolate rich man is followed by Peter saying to Jesus, 'Look, we have left everything and followed you' (Mark 10.28; Matthew 19.27). Luke tones down his words a little by having him say, 'Look, we have left our homes and followed you' (18.28). Jesus royally commends them, and in Luke's version says,

> Truly I tell you, there is no one who has left house or wife or brothers or parents or children, for the sake of the kingdom of God, who will not get back very much more in this age, and in the age to come eternal life.   (18.29–30)

Luke is the only one of the three Evangelists to include wives in the list. By doing that he implies Jesus is addressing only Peter and the other male disciples. It is a rare case of them coming in for Jesus' praise, but Joanna, who deserves it even more, is left out. She has generally been left out ever since, *her* gospel consigned to a silence that only a few such as Richard Bauckham have even noticed, a gospel leaving but a few traces of its existence in just one of the Gospels.

A tale of two sisters: Luke

We will devote the rest of this chapter to three tales. They concern the sisters Martha and Mary. Again we have their names. We know what to call them, and that makes it easier to imagine them as flesh and blood and to speak of their humanity. One of their stories appears in Luke, the other two in John. First Luke's:

> Now as they [Jesus and his disciples] went on their way, he entered a certain village, where a woman named Martha welcomed him into her home. She had a sister named Mary, who sat at the Lord's feet and listened to what he was saying. But Martha was distracted by her many tasks; so she came to him and asked, 'Lord, do you not care that my sister has left me to do all the work by myself? Tell her then to help me.' But the Lord answered her, 'Martha, Martha, you are worried and distracted by many things; there is need of only one thing. Mary has chosen the better part, which will not be taken away from her.'   (Luke 10.38–42)

A revealing passage, indeed. When John speaks of Martha and Mary, he will locate them in Bethany, a village just outside Jerusalem. Luke's Jesus has already 'set his face to go to Jerusalem' (9.51), but in chapter 10 he is nowhere near the city. The difference matters little, for there remain significant similarities between the portrayals of the sisters in the two Gospels. In both of them Martha has the greater authority; presumably she is the older woman. In both she is the more assertive, though Mary will turn out to be more insightful than her. In John they have a brother, Lazarus, but he remains in the shadows of the narrative even after Jesus brings him back to life; till then he is located in the pitch black of death and the tomb. There are no other men mentioned in any of the tales, no father, no husbands. In Luke Martha appears to be the owner of the house, the head of the household.

The prominence of the two women in the stories can be partly explained by their setting. Luke's story and the second one in John are located inside the home, and we are speaking of a culture where to a large extent the home was regarded as the sphere of women, while men made sure they dominated the public space. John's second passage about the sisters is set outdoors, but there the context is the burial of their brother, and women played a significant role in mourning the dead. In that respect, therefore, Luke and John do not challenge the cultural expectations of women and men, or the fundamental restrictions imposed upon women because of their gender. However, what they report is still remarkable, not least the intimacy between the sisters and Jesus.

This, indeed, is the most significant similarity between Luke's and John's accounts. The two women are portrayed as close friends of his, and generous ones, too. They offer him hospitality, and in John his other disciples as well; when they address Jesus, Martha in Luke and both she and Mary in John exhibit a plainness of speech that betokens intimacy. I once explored the ways in which Moses is portrayed and how he speaks to God in his first encounter at the Burning Bush in Exodus 3–4, and in his more mature prayers of Exodus 5.22–23 and Numbers 11.10–15. In those later prayers he uses, so I suggested, 'the language of the lover to the beloved, the language of the blazing row, employed by those who feel they have been grievously let down'.[22] Now we have to be careful here! In making a comparison between Martha and Mary and Moses, I am *not* suggesting that Jesus was the women's lover, any more than God and Moses were lovers! And in the stories of the sisters we do not meet with a blazing row, either, though we do find anger, hurt and feelings of being seriously let down. What I was emphasizing in my discussion of Moses was his closeness to God as the one to whom God used to speak 'face to face' (Exodus 33.11) and the way that astonishing intimacy is reflected in the blunt speech of his own prayer. There is no one closer to God than Moses in the Old Testament. So when we hear Martha burst into the room in Luke's story and complain to Jesus, 'Lord, do you not care that my sister has left me to do all the work by myself?' or when we observe how she and her sister speak to Jesus in John, we find ourselves asking the question, 'Is there anyone in the Gospels closer to Jesus than these women?' At the very least their way of talking to him is striking and significant.

The same can be said of Jesus' responses. 'Martha, Martha,' he says to her in Luke. When God first addresses Moses at the Burning Bush, he calls to him out of the bush, 'Moses, Moses' (Exodus 3.4). The double use of his name there reveals the urgency of the situation, but also whispers of the depth of friendship between them that is to come. In Luke's Gospel there is only one other occasion, that of the Last Supper, where Jesus uses someone's name twice over, 'Simon, Simon, listen!' (22.31). In Acts, in the thrice-told story of Paul meeting the risen Jesus on the road to Damascus, Luke will speak of

Jesus calling out to him, 'Saul, Saul' (Acts 9.4, 22.7, 26.14). Those are the only examples of the double name in the whole of Luke's long, two-volume work. In John, when Mary chides him and breaks down in front of him, Jesus bursts into tears.

Why does Martha in Luke invite Jesus into her home? We are not given the back story. Is this the first time Jesus has met the sisters? How much have they heard about him? Is Martha's offer of hospitality an impulsive gesture, or have she and Mary been eagerly awaiting Jesus' arrival in their village? Luke does not allow us to answer these questions. If we imagine this as their first meeting, then Mary is at once bowled over. She 'sat at the Lord's feet and listened to what he was saying' (10.39). 'Mary thus assumes the role of a disciple,' comments Loveday Alexander: 'what else, after all, does a disciple do?'[23] The very word 'disciple' and its Greek equivalent in the Gospels means one who learns, and Mary is keen to learn. Luke may not call her a disciple, but there she is, sitting at Jesus' feet, listening to him, learning.

Does that mean Martha is *not* a disciple? For many, and not just women as I can testify, this is an unsettling story, as far as Martha is concerned. She and Jesus are the main characters in the passage. Martha welcomes him into *her* home. *She* speaks to Jesus; Mary does not. Jesus replies to *her*; he only talks *about* Mary. And yet it is Martha who appears to be rebuked. Does this story then reinforce the notion of the good little woman who sits and learns and keeps her mouth shut, while the woman who dares open her mouth is effectively silenced? Is Jesus telling Martha to sit down and shut up? And women's work, the work of providing hospitality, the work of preparing a meal and serving a guest, does that all count for nothing? Is there something *wrong* with it? Surely Martha's complaint is entirely justified. She needs Mary's help, and Jesus should not need to have it pointed out. When it is, he should tell Mary to leave the circle at once, should he not? Instead he says, 'Mary has chosen the better part.' Well, that seems clear enough. Women can be disciples, so long as they join a man's world, leaving the other women in the lurch doing work that represents 'the worse part'.

But wait. If we translate the Greek of 10.40 more literally, we have Luke telling us that Martha is distracted by 'much serving', and 'serving' in Luke is *good*! Serving is of the essence. It is what the disciples are called to do, and it helps define who Jesus is. We have already quoted his saying at the Last Supper, 'I am among you as one who serves' (Luke 22.27).

Immediately before Luke's story of Martha and Mary we find the Parable of the Good Samaritan. That has many dimensions to it, but it is clearly about serving. The Samaritan traveller does not stop to tell the Jew lying by the roadside how very sorry he is to see him in that state and then move on. He tends his wounds, lifts him onto his animal, takes him to an inn, looks after him for the night and pays the innkeeper enough to give him lodging until he is fully recovered. At the end of the parable Jesus famously says, 'Go and do likewise' (10.37). Discipleship means both learning and doing. Jesus was a Jew, after all, and for him discipleship could not mean anything else.

At the start of chapter 10 Luke has another passage unique to his Gospel, about Jesus sending ahead as many as 70 of his followers to the towns and villages he is intending to visit. 'I am sending you out like lambs into the midst of wolves,' he tells them.

> Whatever house you enter, first say, 'Peace to this house!' and if anyone is there who shares in peace, your peace will rest upon that person . . . Whenever you enter a town and its people welcome you, eat what is set before you; cure the sick who are there, and say to them, 'The kingdom of God has come near to you.'　　　(10.3, 5–6a, 8–9)

By that token, as Warren Carter observes, in welcoming Jesus into her home, 'Martha is a child of peace, who has encountered God's reign.' Her welcome is more than an act of generous hospitality. It denotes her embracing Jesus' mission, and supporting it.[24]

So Martha too must be seen as a disciple. Between them the two sisters are fulfilling the demands of discipleship, the learning and the doing. Why then does Jesus say to Martha, 'Mary has chosen the better part'? Because, as the poet of Ecclesiastes puts it so beautifully, 'For everything there is a season, and a time for every matter under heaven' (Ecclesiastes 3.1), and this is not the time for doing. Jesus is going up to Jerusalem, and twice already he has warned his other disciples that he is going to be put to death. 'If any want to become my followers, let them deny themselves and take up their cross daily and follow me' (9.23). Both sisters need to understand this, and much else besides. On the Jericho road, in the parable, it was the time for doing. For Martha and Mary, with Jesus sitting in their house, it is the time for listening. As Loveday Alexander remarks, this passage gives us 'the story of a hostess who "misses the point" of her hospitable activity'.[25] Jesus tells Martha she is 'worried and distracted by many things'. We human beings all worry from time to time, and much anxiety is perfectly reasonable and sometimes essential. It is a question of pre-occupations and priorities. On this occasion, paradoxically, Martha's preoccupations and priorities and her very busyness prevent her from *doing* what the particular occasion demands, sitting at Jesus' feet and listening – and chipping in and questioning and arguing, no doubt. But she is still a disciple, a child of peace, a friend of Jesus, and one who is within Jesus' innermost circle: 'Martha, Martha,' he calls her. In that repeating of her name we catch the sound of deep affection.

A tale of two sisters: John

John's introduction of Martha and Mary seems rather clumsy: 'Now a certain man was ill, Lazarus of Bethany, the village of Mary and her sister Martha. Mary was the one who anointed the Lord with perfume and wiped his feet with her hair; her brother Lazarus was ill' (John 11.1–2). This might suggest the following story is going to be about Lazarus. Its plot does centre on his death and burial, but as the story proceeds, we see it is mainly about the two sisters. John himself hints as much, when he describes Bethany as their village. We notice also that John here puts Mary first, but that is only because he anticipates a story yet to come, the story of the anointing. A few verses later he speaks of 'Martha and her sister', and thereafter Martha will always come first. Nevertheless, John strikes a balance in his treatment of the two women and the roles they play, which is greater than the one we found in Luke.

For a start, when Lazarus falls ill, both sisters together send a message to Jesus, 'Lord, he whom you love is ill' (11.3). That description of Lazarus is very interesting, of course, and two verses later John will speak of Jesus' love for 'Martha and her sister and Lazarus', reassuring us that his love is not confined to the brother. John's Gospel has a good deal about 'love', more than any of the others. 'I give you a new commandment,' Jesus says to his disciples, 'that you love one another. Just as I have loved you, you also should love one another' (13.34). Earlier in that chapter John says, 'Having loved his own who were in the world, he loved them to the end' (13.1b). Yet still, beyond Martha, Mary and Lazarus, the mysterious disciple 'whom he loved' is the only individual picked out for this special honour. The peculiarly close friendship between Jesus and the sisters that we found in Luke is here underlined, and extended to their brother.

Clearly this passage *does* have a back story. It is possible to think of Martha and Mary in Luke 10 as meeting Jesus for the first time. Not so in John 11. Their relationship with him is already established, and indeed has become a deep and significant one. We might think it strange that John has not mentioned them before. Yet that is how he writes. In his stories of the resurrection he gives pride of place to Mary of Magdala. Nothing in the earlier chapters of his Gospel prepares us for that, as we have already noted. Even at the cross Mary is but a name in a list of witnesses, and the last name to boot. Those who first heard John's Gospel being performed in their community no doubt were familiar with other stories about all three women. They would once have been well-known figures, well known for the leadership they exercised in the Church as it began and for the compelling stories they told.

John 11 does not, of course, give this particular story of the two sisters and their brother in anything like its raw state (whatever that might have been). 'The Jesus of John spends most of the Gospel discussing himself.' So says Diarmaid MacCulloch.[26] It is a brilliant remark, and it highlights one of the chief differences between John and the other Gospels. Jesus speaks with another voice in John. None of the Gospels give us the actual words of Jesus. They are all written in Greek, for starters, and Jesus spoke Aramaic, a very different language, closely related to Hebrew. To engage with a Semitic language is to enter another world, as anyone who has read Old Testament texts in Hebrew will testify. Yet in Mark, Matthew and Luke it is sometimes *as if* we can hear Jesus speaking and even catch his Galilean accent, not just in some of the pithy and memorable sayings, such as, 'So the last will be first, and the first will be last' (Matthew 20.16), but in some of the more radical stories we call parables. In John that voice is missing and is replaced by another, that of John himself. All four Evangelists have shaped the traditions to their own ends, but John takes that reshaping to a different level. From the Prologue to the end of his Gospel he gives us his meditation on Jesus.

It is a meditation of enormous profundity, and some of us Christians would say it can sometimes take us deeper into the heart of things, the heart of the Truth that Jesus both proclaimed and represented, than the other three Gospels. In particular it can be argued that John gives us a clearer picture than the others of the place women played in the life and ministry of Jesus. His stories of Martha and Mary are a case in point. They do not feature in Mark or Matthew at all, though both suggest Jesus was given hospitality by some family in Bethany after his fateful grand entrance into Jerusalem (Mark 11.11–12; Matthew 21.17). And John devotes much more space to them than Luke does, and gives both of them a voice. Nevertheless, it is clear, when we turn to John's narrative, that the two women are the servants of John's theology, and to their hurt.

We have already quoted John 11.1–3. Let us resume the story at verse 4:

> But when Jesus heard it, he said, 'This illness does not lead to death; rather it is for God's glory, so that the Son of God may be glorified through it.' Accordingly, though Jesus loved Martha and her sister and Lazarus, after having heard that Lazarus was ill, he stayed two days longer in the place where he was.   (11.4–6)

So now we know what John is interested in: glorifying Jesus. How much Martha and Mary (and Lazarus, too) will have to sacrifice to that cause is already hinted at and will soon become clear.

'Then after this he said to the disciples, "Let us go to Judea again." The disciples said to him, "Rabbi, the Jews were just now trying to stone you, and are you going there again?" ' (11.7–8). This reminds us of the negative portrayal of the male disciples we have already encountered in the other Gospels (and also, alas, of John's habit of demonizing 'the Jews'). If it were left to these disciples to decide, Jesus would not go south and the story would come to an abrupt end. Jesus' reply to them is an example of John and his Jesus at their most cryptic (11.9–10), but we can see clearly enough that Jesus does not share their sense of danger, nor is he to be deflected from his purpose. 'Our friend Lazarus has fallen asleep, but I am going there to awaken him' (11.11). The disciples misunderstand and take his words literally. Jesus has to abandon metaphor and speak more plainly: 'Lazarus is dead. For your sake I am glad I was not there, so that you may believe. But let us go to him' (11.14b–15). So Jesus, who knows through divine insight that Lazarus has died (for no one has told him), is glad he was not there. Lazarus' sisters will not be so sanguine, or seem so unfeeling.

> When Jesus arrived, he found that Lazarus had already been in the tomb for four days. Now Bethany was near Jerusalem, some two miles away, and many of the Jews had come to Martha and Mary to console them about their brother. When Martha heard that Jesus was coming, she went and met him, while Mary stayed at home. Martha said to Jesus, 'Lord, if you had been here, my brother would not have died. But even now I know that God will give you whatever you ask of him.'   (11.17–22)

Many commentators pick up on the detail of Lazarus having been dead for four days (people then were buried on the day they died). It would have made no difference, they say, if Jesus had set out as soon as he got the message from the sisters that Lazarus was ill. Their brother was almost certainly dead by the time it reached him. But John's narrative is not as straightforward as that. John needs to delay Jesus' arrival, so that he can do justice, as he sees it, to his divine power, so he can be sufficiently 'glorified'. As Raymond Brown explains, 'There was an opinion among the rabbis that the soul hovered near the body for three days but after that there was no hope of resuscitation.'[27] As John will tell us when eventually we reach Lazarus' tomb, his corpse has begun to decompose. That serves to underline the significance of Jesus' delay. By the time he gets to Bethany, there is, according to the beliefs of the time, no hope left. Had he set out immediately there would have been. Indeed, Martha says, 'my brother would not have died', and her sister will soon say the same. We cannot read the commentators and then tell the two women they are wrong. There is an unresolved tension in the narrative. The sisters are to be believed and their voices heard. We must listen to their grief and take note of their complaint. 'If you had been here, my brother would not have died.' John attempts to divert our attention from the rawness of Martha's speech by having her continue with, 'But even now I know that God will give you whatever you ask of him.' Her piety is not convincing. Her grief, her anger, her veiled accusation are. Had Jesus come straightaway, he could have prevented her brother's death; he could have healed him from his illness. That is surely what she means. But he waited, he waited *two days*, and now Lazarus is dead and all hope has died with him! That is what her words convey.

And that is too uncomfortable for us to dwell on, so John immediately takes our arm and leads us away into theological discourse, to Jesus discussing himself.

> Jesus said to her, 'Your brother will rise again.' Martha said to him, 'I know that he will rise again in the resurrection on the last day.' Jesus said to her, 'I am the resurrection and the life. Those who believe in me, even though they die, will live, and everyone who lives and believes in me will never die. Do you believe this?' She said to him, 'Yes, Lord, I believe that you are the Messiah, the Son of God, the one coming into the world.' (11.23–27)

That is one of the most famous passages in John's Gospel. So is this (I shall keep to the NRSV, but put it into short lines, for it is exalted poetry):

In the beginning was the Word,
and the Word was with God,
and the Word was God.
He was in the beginning with God.
All things came into being through him,
and without him not one thing came into being.
What has come into being in him was life,
and the life was the light of all people.
The light shines in the darkness,
and the darkness did not overcome it.   (1.1–5)

The opening words of the Prologue. The opening words of the Gospel. All else is commentary. Those shimmering lines lead to two great climaxes in John's great narrative: the raising of Lazarus, which brings to a conclusion the first part of the Gospel, and the rising of Jesus himself, which concludes the whole. John Pilch points out that the word 'life' appears 47 times in John, while only 6 times in Matthew, 3 times in Mark and 5 in Luke. In John 'Jesus' works or signs,' he says, 'are all about life.'[28]

There are other passages in John, beyond the Prologue, which prepare us for the story in chapter 11. John includes seven miracles, or 'signs'. The raising of Lazarus is the last. The second of them has a 'royal official' approach Jesus, begging him to come down with him to Capernaum to heal his son, who is at the point of death. Jesus' response anticipates his delaying those two days before he sets off for Bethany, and seems intolerably harsh, if not cruel: 'Jesus said to him, "Unless you see signs and wonders you will not believe." The official said to him, "Sir, come down before my little boy dies." Jesus said to him, "Go; your son will live" ' (4.48–49). 'Come down before my little boy dies.' Through his own plain-speaking the little boy's father has to release the divine compassion, which at first seems locked up in a tight theological safe. 'If you had been here, my brother would not have died.' When Martha's sister Mary gets to say those words, she will at last bring Jesus to his senses, and set free his tears.

The raising of Lazarus leads straight into 'the chief priests and the Pharisees' calling a meeting of the Jewish council to plot how to bring an end to Jesus. That passage includes the infamous remark of Caiaphas, the high priest, 'it is better for you to have one man die for the people than to have the whole nation destroyed' (11.50). When first we are told that the 'Jews started persecuting Jesus' because of what he was doing, Jesus tells them in the course of his reply,

> just as the Father raises the dead and gives them life, so also the Son gives life to whomever he wishes . . . just as the Father has life in himself, so he has granted the Son also to have life in himself . . . the hour is coming when all who are in their graves will hear his voice and will come out. (5.21, 26, 28b–29a)

After this it would seem easy to agree with Mona West when she describes the conversation between Martha and Jesus as 'the story's theological heart' and says, '[I]t transforms Martha into a believer in Jesus as the resurrection and the life . . . her words articulate her faith in Jesus as the one who gives life.'[29] In truth, John's narrative is once again not that simple. When finally Jesus reaches Lazarus' tomb, Martha will say, 'Lord, already there is a stench because he has been dead four days' (11.39b). Theological discussion has not, it seems, taken her as far in her journey towards the truth as her confession about Jesus being the Messiah and the Son of God might suggest. Of course not. She needs to *see*, to see death conquered, to see her brother again. But first she must fetch her sister Mary.

> She went back and called her sister Mary, and told her privately, 'The Teacher is here and is calling for you.' And when she heard it, she got up quickly and went to him. Now Jesus had not yet come to the village, but was still at the place where Martha had met him . . . When Mary came where Jesus was and saw him, she knelt at his feet and said to him, 'Lord, if you had been here, my brother would not have died.' When Jesus saw her weeping, and the Jews who came with her also weeping, he was greatly disturbed in spirit and deeply moved. He said, 'Where have you laid him?' They said to him, 'Lord, come and see.' Jesus began to weep. (11.28–35)

This conforms to the pictures of the two sisters painted by Luke. She is the quiet one, the one who sits, and here the one who waits. And still Jesus waits, also! Martha runs back home, but Jesus does not move. Two days he stayed up in Galilee. Now he stays outside the village. He is calling for Mary, so Martha says. Why does he not go to Mary herself, and then run with her and Martha to their brother's tomb? Is John meaning to emphasize Jesus' authority, when he has him stand stock still and summon Mary to his presence? If so, he does so at the expense of Jesus' compassion and his friendship.

Martha's meeting with Jesus, as John reports it, carries mixed messages. The same is true of Mary's. She kneels at Jesus' feet (as she will do again in chapter 12), as if she is more deferential than her sister, but her speech is blunt, more so than Martha's. 'Lord, if you had been here, my brother would not have died.' She repeats Martha's words almost exactly. (John makes one tiny change in the order of the words in the Greek. On such small variations great literature thrives, but it is of no consequence for the sense of what Mary says.) And there she stops. No 'I know that God will give you whatever you ask of him.' No theology, just grief and hurt, anger no doubt, accusation and profound disappointment, disappointment in Jesus. She thought their friendship meant more than this, this despair, this death.

Martha's speech moved Jesus to theological discourse. Mary's moves him to tears (what a shame the NRSV does not convey the terseness of John's Greek, as the King James Bible does with its simple 'Jesus wept'). It also moves him to a swirl of intense emotion. The single Greek word behind the NRSV's 'greatly disturbed', a verb which John repeats when Jesus reaches Lazarus' tomb, can suggest great anger, as it does when Mark uses it in his story of the anointing, when those present react to the woman's actions (Mark 14.5). Here surely it indicates that Jesus breaks down, collapses into the maelstrom of grief. Anger is of course an almost invariable component of new, raw grief. *So Mary teaches the Teacher how to grieve*. It will not be her last lesson.

Mary's speech also moves Jesus in a more literal way. At last he goes to the tomb.

It was a cave, and a stone was lying against it. Jesus said, 'Take away the stone.' Martha, the sister of the dead man, said to him, 'Lord, already there is a stench because he has been dead four days.' Jesus said to her, 'Did I not tell you that if you believed, you would see the glory of God?' So they took away the stone. And Jesus looked upward and said, 'Father, I thank you for having heard me. I knew that you always hear me, but I have said this for the sake of the crowd standing here, so that they may believe that you sent me.' When he had said this, he cried with a loud voice, 'Lazarus, come out!' The dead man came out, his hands and feet bound with strips of cloth, and his face wrapped in a cloth. Jesus said to them, 'Unbind him, and let him go.'   (11. 38b–44)

In his commentary on John, Mark Stibbe says:

> Jesus stands at the threshold of the tomb of his friend Lazarus. By standing at an entrance associated so obviously with suffering, mourning, sickness and death, Jesus is revealed as the God who is prepared to stand at the most extreme and painful of human experiences . . . He is not some mystical, neo-Platonic God who stands far beyond the harsh realities endured by those trapped within a frail mortality. This Jesus, the Son of God, is the deity who sheds tears, who feels anger, and who dares to look through the dark threshold of a place which he himself will have to enter.[30]

Fine sentiments, and ones which lead us towards the heart of what we Christians mean by the Incarnation. 'The dark threshold of a place which he himself will have to enter.' Yes, John clearly means us to see in the death and raising of Lazarus a sign of what is to come in his narrative, the death, burial and rising of Jesus himself. That will be the moment for John when the glory of God is fully revealed. Here also, by the tomb of Lazarus, we see the glory of God, or so Jesus tells Martha: 'Did I not tell you that if you believed, you would see the glory of God?' But *do* we? Yes, we do. For Jesus does more than dare look into the realm of death, he defeats it, and if he wins this victory then he can surely win any contest with the forces of evil and chaos. So John would have us believe, and it is a belief that underlies all Christian hope. Yet the glory of God, as seen in Jesus of Nazareth, is not revealed just, or even primarily, in his victory over dark forces. It is seen in his compassion and love, and at points in John 11 these seem sorely lacking in Jesus. It is disappointing, to say the least, that when at last he stands at the entrance of the tomb, he should again respond to Martha by retreating into a theological discourse and prayer that distance him from the harsh reality of the sisters' loss and grief. If again we swing the spotlight on the two women and look at *them*, then we see there is a gospel here that is left half told.

A tale of two sisters: John again

It is very interesting to see how John portrays the two sisters in the story we have just explored. Martha is the one who takes the initiative, while Mary is a more passive figure; Jesus engages Martha in dialogue, but not her sister; the women share the message they send at the beginning about their brother's illness, but after that Mary has but one speech, a very short one that repeats almost exactly something her sister has already said. If we count the words in the Greek that John gives them to say, then Martha has 63 to herself, Mary only 10. And yet it is their joint request that (eventually) sets Jesus on his journey south, and it is Mary's ten words that persuade him to take the last vital steps to the mouth of Lazarus' tomb. Though Martha is presented as the more dominant figure in the narrative, Mary would seem to have more influence on Jesus. And while Martha emerges as one who *learns* from Jesus (in other words, as a true disciple), Mary is his *teacher*. The final story about the two women again presents them in those roles, only this time the lesson Jesus learns from Mary is a much more significant one. At long last we have reached John's story of the anointing.

> Six days before the Passover Jesus came to Bethany, the home of Lazarus, whom he had raised from the dead. There they gave a dinner for him. Martha served, and Lazarus was one of those at the table with him. Mary took a pound of costly perfume made of pure nard, anointed Jesus' feet, and wiped them with her hair. The house was filled with the fragrance of the perfume. But Judas Iscariot, one of his disciples (the one who was about to betray him) said, 'Why was this perfume not sold for three hundred denarii and the money given to the poor?' (He said this not because he cared about the poor, but because he was a thief; he kept the common purse and used to steal what was put into it.) Jesus said, 'Leave her alone. She bought it so that she might keep it for the day of my burial. You always have the poor with you, but you do not always have me.' (12.1–8)

In its brevity and lack of theological discourse this might almost be a story from Mark, Matthew or Luke, and of course it shares many features with their stories of the anointing of Jesus. The similarities bear further witness to the strength of the tradition. Stories of a woman or women anointing Jesus must have been told over and over in many of the earliest Christian communities, and their importance recognized.

Was Mary of Bethany herself one of those who first passed it on? Quite possibly, although her name came to be remembered only by the Johannine community, or by those on whom John depended for his narrative.

Like Mark and Matthew, John times the anointing just before the Passover, and with plots to arrest and do away with Jesus swirling round his head. Like the unnamed woman in Mark and Matthew, Mary anoints Jesus in preparation for his burial. But John locates the anointing not in the house of a Simon, whether leper or Pharisee, but in 'the home of Lazarus'. That description is striking given that John began the story in his previous chapter by talking of Bethany as 'the village of Martha and her sister Mary'. The shift can be easily explained. As we have already noted, the raising of Lazarus is for John the final act that stirs the Jewish religious authorities into action and seals Jesus' fate. He tells us that immediately before the anointing, and as soon as it is over the plot will thicken with the chief priests planning to put Lazarus to death as well 'since it was on account of him that many of the Jews were deserting and were believing in Jesus' (12.11). Lazarus, then, is a key character for John in the shaping of his Gospel. That being the case, it is interesting to see what a shadowy figure he remains. The anointing happens in his home, and he is one of those at the meal that his sisters prepare. Beyond that, nothing. He is given no words to say. He does nothing but recline and (presumably) eat. After the opening two verses the spotlight leaves him and he is left in the dark.

'Martha served.' Those words remind us not of the other three stories of the anointing, but of the story of Martha and Mary in Luke 10. But this time her service provokes no discussion nor is the cause for any concern. The echoes of that passage in Luke together with John's putting her name first might suggest this story is again going to pay her more attention than her sister. The next verse focuses on Mary, however, and Martha will not be mentioned again. This is *Mary's* story.

Except in some ways it isn't. The passage spends more time on Judas Iscariot than on her. She has just one verse devoted to her near the start, and one more just before the end. She has nothing to say. The middle of the story is dominated by some particularly nasty material on Judas. Clearly John and his community had never forgiven Judas for his betraying Jesus. As if betrayal was not enough, they take delight into turning him into a thief, accusing him of raiding the common purse, the one to which Joanna and the others were contributing. The other Gospels do not demonize him to that extent, even if Luke in Acts 1.18 goes into the gory details of his death. In blaming Judas here John is closest to Matthew's version of the anointing, where it is 'the disciples' who get angry with the woman and 'the waste' of her perfume. In Luke 7 it is Simon the host who is so displeased, though for different reasons, while Mark speaks more vaguely of 'some of those who were there'. Nevertheless, in other respects John's account is most reminiscent of Mark's. They describe the perfume in almost exactly the same way, using the term 'nard', and they put the same price on it, 300 denarii. John's words to Judas, 'let her alone', are the same as the ones used by Mark, except in his case the verb is in the plural because more than one person is being addressed. Both include, together with Matthew in this case, the saying, 'You always have the poor with you, but you do not always have me.' (In all three versions the wording in the Greek is almost identical.) It is as if John has taken Mark's story, or the tradition he followed, added the material about Judas, identified the woman concerned as Mary of Bethany, and then made one further alteration. Instead of anointing Jesus' head, Mary anoints his feet.

That last detail, of such fundamental importance, as soon we shall see, ties John's version in with Luke's. Yet in almost every other respect John's is a very different tale from Luke's. If he knew of Luke's version, then he took from it the one detail of the anointing of the feet and discarded the rest. It still seems he based his story on Mark's, or on a tradition very close to Mark's, and deliberately change head to feet. Why should he do that? The answer is in his very next chapter.

Now before the festival of the Passover, Jesus knew that his hour had come to depart from this world and go to the Father. Having loved his own who were in the world, he loved them to the end. The devil had already put it into the heart of Judas son of Simon Iscariot to betray him. And during supper Jesus . . . got up from the table, took off his outer robe, and tied a towel around himself. Then he poured water into a basin and began to wash the disciples' feet and to wipe them with the towel that was tied around him . . . After he had washed their feet, and had put on his robe, and had returned to the table, he said to them, 'Do you know what I have done to you? You call me Teacher and Lord – and you are right, for that is what I am. So if I, your Lord and

Teacher, have washed your feet, you also ought to wash one another's feet. For I have set you an example, that you also should do as I have done to you . . . If you know these things, you are blessed if you do them.'   (13.1–5, 12–15, 17)

This is a defining moment in Jesus' ministry. 'You know that among the Gentiles,' Jesus tells his disciples in Mark,

those whom they recognize as their rulers lord it over them, and their great ones are tyrants over them. But it is not so among you; but whoever wishes to become great among you must be your servant, and whoever wishes to be first among you must be slave of all. For the Son of Man came not to be served but to serve, and to give his life as a ransom for many.   (10.42–45)

Luke's version of this passage, which we quoted earlier, ends with, 'For who is greater, the one who is at table or the one who serves? Is it not the one at the table? But I am among you as one who serves' (22.27). Actions speak louder than words. In washing the feet of the ones he loves at this Last Supper Jesus is acting the part of a slave, and more specifically the part of a slave-girl, who is at the bottom of the domestic pecking order in the houses of the rich and powerful. Service takes us to the heart of who Jesus was and to the heart of the realm of God he preached. Only one thing that Jesus does in the Gospels speaks louder about who he is than this act of footwashing, and that is his spreading wide his arms on a cross.

Two particular features of the narratives link the footwashing in John 13 with Mary of Bethany's anointing Jesus' feet. In each case the setting is a meal with Jesus reclining at table with friends; both passages tell of Judas Iscariot. John introduces us to Judas back in 6.70–71, where he describes him as 'a devil' and says that he will betray Jesus. But the anointing story is the first time we have heard of him since then, and the footwashing is the second.

Other details remind us of the earlier story of Martha and Mary in chapter 11. First Martha says to her sister, 'The Teacher is here.' Jesus is described as a teacher in John 1.38 (two disciples address Jesus as 'Rabbi', and John explains the word means teacher); again in 3.2 Nicodemus says to Jesus, 'Rabbi, we know that you are a teacher who has come from God.' Neither of those passages uses 'Teacher' as a title in the way Martha does in 11.28. It is not for nothing that the NRSV translates the word with a capital letter. In only one other place before 11.28 does it appear as a title, and that is in the course of the story of Jesus and the woman caught in adultery (8.4), but this passage is missing from the best and most ancient manuscripts, while other manuscripts have it in different places in John or even in Luke. Scholars have long agreed that the passage was not originally a part of the Gospel that John wrote. So Martha's referring to Jesus as 'the Teacher' is very striking. And where next does it appear in John's narrative? In 13.13, where Jesus says, 'You call me Teacher and Lord.' More literally the Greek has, 'You call me *the* Teacher', exactly as in Martha's speech to Mary. Second, we will recall that in 11.3 the sisters, in their message to Jesus, refer to their brother as 'he whom you love', while in verse 5 John tells us, 'Jesus loved Martha and her sister and Lazarus.' In a part of chapter 11 we did not quote earlier the Jews mourning Lazarus' death see Jesus weeping and exclaim, 'See how he loved him!' (11.36). At the beginning of the story of Jesus performing the footwashing John remarks, 'Having loved his own who were in the world, he loved them to the end' (13.1b).

But of course the most important link between the stories of the two sisters and Jesus' footwashing is their relative proximity. Mary uses expensive perfume and Jesus uses water. Mary is preparing Jesus for his burial, so John's Jesus tells us in 12.7, while Jesus is performing a thoroughly mundane act, even if he is doing it in a quite extraordinary way. Yet when we come to the footwashing in chapter 13, we cannot help but recall what Mary has done in chapter 12. And the details of John's writing we have just explored make plain that he means us to remember it. *And Mary gets there first!*

For the second time, therefore, and in an act of supreme significance, Mary teaches the Teacher. Earlier in chapter 11 she teaches Jesus to engage fully with the reality of death and loss, to share in the grief and pain that surround him, to open his tear ducts and cry. In chapter 12 she shows him what love and devotion mean; she shows him how to love. And she demonstrates what being Messiah and Son of God means. Her sister gives Jesus those titles in 11.27, when she is beginning to learn who he is. But we saw in that same chapter, when she and Jesus reach Lazarus' tomb Martha still has much to learn. At 11.27 the truth for her has not sunk in. Mary in her anointing of Jesus shows that the truth of Jesus has penetrated to the depths of her soul. She shows Jesus that if he is to be Messiah, the Son of God, the Word who was in the beginning with God, the Word who is God, then he must wash feet. In a famous passage in the First Letter of John, the author writes, 'God is love,' and then goes on to say, 'We love because he first loved us' (1 John 4.16b,19). After the story of the footwashing in John 13 we might ourselves say, if we are Christians, 'We serve, because he first served us.' And if we think of Mary and her anointing, then we could add, 'And he served, because she first served him.'

Nowhere in any of the Gospels does a male disciple, let alone one of the Twelve, play such a role as Mary of Bethany here.

Are we to imagine Mary, Martha and Lazarus as among those sharing that last meal with Jesus in chapter 13? Can we imagine Jesus washing *their* feet, too? ? The answer from John is unclear. 'He began to wash the disciples' feet,' he writes, and he makes several more references to 'the disciples' or 'his disciples' in the course of his account of the meal. As we have already discussed, it seems when the Evangelists, including John, speak of 'the disciples', they are thinking only of the men among them. And yet the echoes of 'love' and the way 13.1b reminds us of 11.3, 5 and 36 take us back to Bethany. Furthermore, Jesus' describing Lazarus as 'our friend' in 11.11 is picked up in the language of 15.13–15, where three times he calls those sharing the meal with him his 'friends'. John does not restrict the Last Supper to the Twelve, or to the apostles, as the other Evangelists appear to do. He leaves the door to the room wider open than Mark does, or Matthew and Luke. Martha and Mary are not mentioned in the story of Jesus' footwashing or in the long discourse that follows it. 'The beloved disciple' is (John talks of him reclining next to Jesus in 13.23 and 25), and some commentators, picking up the links between the Last Supper passage and chapter 11, identify that disciple with Lazarus.[31] Others prefer to respect his anonymity and to think of him as someone whom John never names in his Gospel but who was well known to his readers or hearers.[32] Whatever side of that particular fence we choose to stand on, Martha and Mary remain in the deep shadows of the narrative, and there they stay right through to the end of the Gospel.

Peter is more visible and more audible, too. When Jesus comes to wash his feet he asks, 'Lord, are you going to wash my feet?' 'You do not know now what I am doing,' Jesus replies, 'but later you will understand.' Peter protests, vigorously, 'You will never wash my feet!' 'Unless I wash you,' Jesus tells him, 'you have no share with me.' And Peter then responds, 'Lord, not my feet only, but my hands and my head' (13.6–9). Peter does not get it. Even at the end of that little dialogue he still does not understand, and Jesus has to explain further what he is doing. To that John does not record Peter's response.

Mary and no doubt Martha also, if we imagine them being present, need no explanation. They know exactly what Jesus is doing. After all, Mary has taught Jesus what it is!

Concluding reflections

Matthew, Mark, Luke and John: four Gospels; four men. Indeed, there are no books in the New Testament written by women. Any suggestion that there are is but wishful thinking. (The same cannot be said about the Old Testament, where a scholarly case can be made for female authorship of the Song of Songs, Ruth and Proverbs 1–9, for significant traces of women's texts in Lamentations and elsewhere, and where women's songs are occasionally included in the narratives of other books – such as the Song of Miriam in Exodus 15 or the Song of Deborah in Judges 5.[33])

We have to be somewhat cautious, however, in the presumptions we might make about the extent of the male bias in the Gospels. As Bauckham points out,

> male authors can adopt a more or less authentically female voice . . . In the ancient world this was partly because skilled and sensitive oral storytellers, as the evangelists surely were, when relating to a mixed audience, often in situations allowing a degree of audience participation, learn to portray characters with whom their female auditors can identify.[34]

He further points out that while the writers of the Gospels were male, those who had a hand in forming the Gospel traditions no doubt included women as well as men. In our own discussion, we have suggested evidence for such a belief. 'It is also the case,' he says, 'that relatively spare narratives like those in the Gospels, which outline and suggest rather than exclusively portray, can authorize a reader to supply a fuller female perspective than they explicitly express.'[35] That is exactly what I have been trying to do in this chapter and in parts of the first.

All of Bauckham's remarks are very helpful. Nevertheless, we can only dream what the Gospels might have been like had they been written by, let us say, Joanna, Mary of Magdala, Martha and Mary of Bethany as joint authors, and Phoebe, who took Paul's letter to the Romans to the church in Rome, and for whom Paul clearly had huge respect (see Romans 16.1–2). They would no doubt have been very different, and so would the Church. My own Church of England, to which I have belonged all my life, would not have waited till 1994 to ordain women to its priesthood, and another 20 years to consecrate its first woman bishop. Or perhaps, if women had been allowed from the beginning to shape the life of the Church as much as men, they would not have had bishops at all, or at least not seated them on enormous thrones in cathedrals and given them tall, pointy hats to wear!

We must stop daydreaming. The Gospels were not written by women. Yet that makes the nature of the stories about women which they do include – and we have not had time to explore all of them – even more extraordinary. These stories, together with the trenchant and frequent criticism of Jesus' male disciples, point towards a gospel which was never written, but which we can begin to imagine. The hints are there. Might they have something to do with Jesus of Nazareth himself, the kind of man he was, the place occupied by women in his circle, and the honour, admiration and affection he offered them? I have my suspicions.

The women got it. The men so often did not. Each of the male-authored Gospels encourages us to draw that conclusion. It should not be so startling, of course, but after 2,000 years of a male-dominated Church it is. We *need* to be startled by it, and when so much of the mission of the worldwide Church is rightly concerned with the empowerment of women and girls in the wider societies it serves, we need to be very *glad* of it. It can provide a generous, God-given supply of power to our elbow.

3

Rejection rejected . . . and reinstated

What shall we call the parable?

We move now from tales of two sisters to a tale of two brothers. In one respect this one is more typical of the Gospels: there will not be a woman in sight. Our chapter will not range far and wide through all four Gospels, but will restrict itself to Luke and to a single parable of his – with a brief reference at the very end to one short episode in his narrative of Jesus' crucifixion. As we move through the parable, however, we will need to pay much heed to passages in Genesis.

The parable is one of the most famous of all short stories ever told. It is commonly known as the Parable of the Prodigal Son, but that is not a satisfactory title. If we call it that, we will almost certainly be led astray, for there is another son in the story, as we are told right at the beginning. Using the language of drama, we can say there are two acts, and though that other son is invisible in the first, he dominates the second. To call the parable 'The Prodigal Son' is to focus on one son and neglect the other, to pay heed to the first act and either to ignore the second entirely or reduce it to an anti-climax. This, in fact, is precisely what countless preachers and teachers have done in the past, partly because the first act can seem so much more dramatic and appealing than the second. It is vital, however, that we examine the second part as carefully as the first, and pay as much heed to the second brother as to the first. Otherwise we will miss the challenge of the parable and fail to notice its extraordinary punchline. We will simply get it wrong.

So what *shall* we call it? *The HarperCollins Study Bible*, an annotated edition of the NRSV, calls it, 'The Parable of the Prodigal and His Brother'. That is better, but too cumbersome. Kenneth Bailey calls it, 'The Father and the Two Lost Sons'[1] and Klyne Snodgrass, 'The Compassionate Father and His Two Lost Sons'.[2] Both of those titles have great virtue: they remind us of the key role played by the father (in both acts), and prepare us for meeting two lost sons, not just one. But should we be told what to think of the sons before we begin, and should Snodgrass be allowed to sum up the father also in a single word? We need to make up our own minds as we read. And both titles are still very long. Bernard Brandon Scott has, 'A Man Had Two Sons'.[3] That is very neat, and indeed is exactly how Luke's text of the parable begins. It would be good, perhaps, to keep it even simpler and call it, 'The Two Sons', but then we risk confusion with another parable in Matthew 21.28–32 which is commonly given that title. Though Luke's story speaks of 'sons' or 'son', and does not introduce the term 'brother' until the second act, we will choose to call it 'The Two Brothers', and for a particular reason: it focuses more clearly on what becomes a major theme of this story, sibling rivalry.

Luke's parable or Jesus' parable?

In the opening paragraph we described it as one of Luke's parables. That does not mean we believe he composed it himself out of thin air. The vast majority of commentators believe it goes back to Jesus himself, and I am firmly among them. But let us not imagine it is the original version, however much preachers might assume or tell us it is. As James Dunn reminds us, there was no original version.[4] Instead there was an original *event*, a moment when Jesus told this tale to an audience far more used to hearing than reading. He would not have had a script. The Gospels make plain he was a storyteller of consummate skill, and certainly the version we have in Luke 15 is a beautifully crafted piece, where every word counts and the drama is very carefully shaped. But how much of the crafting is Luke's? Maybe very little, though ultimately we cannot answer that question, beyond noting the obvious fact that the text is in Greek, rather than Jesus' Aramaic. Returning to the original event of Jesus' telling, we find Dunn very properly offering words of caution:

> the witnesses would have seen and heard differently; the event or words would have impacted them differently. And their reporting or sharing of that impact would have been different . . . original/originating event is not to be confused with original report of the event.[5]

And Dunn goes on to raise the possibility that Jesus may have told the same parable more than once. In the case of The Two Brothers I would suggest we should think of probability. I have found in my own attempts at preaching through storytelling, a practice I have been following on occasion for nearly 40 years, that I have been able to tell some of the pieces many times, and though I have always had a script, the way I have told them has varied with the circumstances and with the nature of the congregation or gathered group. If I had had a piece remotely as good as The Two Brothers, I would have told it time beyond number! Surely Jesus told it more than once, and if so it would have come out different every time, and each time been heard and received differently by the variety of people there.

To put it simply, what we have *behind* the text is Jesus' parable, and *in* the text Luke's particular Greek performance of it, based on performances he and his particular community had already heard. Since the parable does not appear in any of the other Gospels, Luke's version is all we have, but we can still, as we work our way through his text, speak with confidence of Jesus' own creativity. We just need to remember that when we talk of Jesus saying that or doing this in the story, we are using a measure of shorthand.

Beware being told what to think

The parable leaves a great deal to our imagination, and, except in the introduction Luke provides and at the very end, we are not told what to think. That is a good sign. It puts the parable among the finest and most profound examples of storytelling in the Bible. The writers of the Garden of Eden story in Genesis 2–3, for example, or the Binding of Isaac in Genesis 22 do not tell us what to make of them. They leave that up to us, and that is one of the reasons why they have continued to fascinate and enthral us for well over two millennia. Of course plenty of people have come along during those centuries and told us exactly what they mean, and of those many have ruined them in the process, ignoring the ambiguities and delicate nuances of the Hebrew. The Garden of Eden story has suffered more than most, being left knee-deep in a misogyny it does not contain.[6] The Evangelists, at least Mark, Matthew and Luke himself, generally follow the example of the Old Testament writers. They leave many questions unanswered, many connections for us to find, and mercifully they tend to avoid trying to give us 'the message' of a piece. They use their considerable creative powers to draw us into the little worlds of their stories and discover for ourselves just how large those worlds are. They mean us to be not informed, but inspired, challenged, changed. In that regard they remain true not just to their Jewish Scriptures but, as far as we can see, to Jesus himself. For the Gospels make it plain enough Jesus was not prescriptive in his teaching. He was a poet and a storyteller, who taught through pithy poetic sayings and through parables. He left his words ringing in the ears of his hearers. He did not interpret them. He too wished not to inform but to enthral, inspire, challenge, change. Where we do find his words interpreted for us in the Gospels, they are invariably spoiled or left impoverished. Amy-Jill Levine, in her brilliant book on the parables, says of the Parable of the Widow and the Judge in Luke 18.2–5, for example, 'Luke turns the parable into an allegory, and so *platitude replaces provocation*'[7] (my italics).

It may well be that Luke has interfered with the very end of The Two Brothers. We will discuss that possibility more fully when we come to it, but he appears in the last verse to come close to telling us what the parable is about, and closer still to spoiling its punchline.

Beware the scribes and the Pharisees! Or should we?

Luke's attempt to interpret the parable for us is even clearer in the introduction he gives it. He begins a new section in his narrative with this: 'Now all the tax-collectors and sinners were coming near to listen to him. And the Pharisees and the scribes were grumbling and saying, "This fellow welcomes sinners and eats with them" ' (Luke 15.1–2). The parables of The Lost Sheep, The Lost Coin and The Two Brothers follow immediately upon these words. We have to be very careful here, for Luke is using damaging stereotypes.

Levine reminds us of how Paul instructs the Christian community at Corinth in 1 Corinthians 5.11:

> But now I am writing to you not to associate with anyone who bears the name of brother or sister who is sexually immoral or greedy, or is an idolater, reviler, drunkard, or robber. Do not even eat with such a one.

Then she continues:

> They are the ancient drug pushers, insider traders, arms dealers, and, especially colonial collaborationists. And yes, Jesus eats with them – that's part of his genius, that he recognizes that they are part of the community and he goes out to get them.[8]

Paul's comment in 1 Corinthians is itself evidence that Jesus' table fellowship and the kind of people he welcomed into his circle continued to be problematic for some early Christians, including some Christian Jews, like Paul himself. No doubt it troubled some of Jesus' fellow Jews during his lifetime. But we should treat Luke's reference to the Pharisees and scribes with great caution, for there is no doubt they are demonized in the Gospels.

There were some among them, after all, who were sympathetic towards Jesus, and if John is to be believed, some who became his disciples. In Luke 13.31 'some Pharisees' warn Jesus that Herod is out to kill him, and tell him to leave the region where he is. As we saw in our first chapter, Luke also has a story about a Pharisee named Simon who asks Jesus to eat with him (7.36–50), and in 14.1–6 he has another, about 'a leader of the Pharisees', no less, who invites him to his house to share a meal on the Sabbath. Most remarkably of all, John devotes a lengthy passage (3.1–21) to a Pharisee called Nicodemus, who comes to Jesus by night and begins by saying, 'Rabbi, we know that you are a teacher who has come from God' (3.2). John has Jesus speak in reply of Nicodemus' lack of comprehension (3.10)[9] and say to him, 'you lot' (the 'you' in the Greek is plural) 'do not receive our testimony' (3.11b). To that John gives Nicodemus no opportunity to respond, and we are left at the end of the passage with Jesus' hostile words ringing in our ears. Yet this is not the last we hear of Nicodemus. Suddenly, without warning, after the story of Jesus' crucifixion, he reappears, this time with a Joseph of Arimathea, a man we have not heard of before, but who we now learn is 'a disciple' of Jesus. Together Joseph and Nicodemus ask Pilate to release Jesus' body for burial. That itself is a brave thing to do, but they are successful, and they give him a burial fit for an emperor, using, so John tells us, 100 pounds of myrrh and aloes (19.38–42). Their extravagance reminds us straightaway of Mary of Bethany in John 12.3, or the nard or myrrh used by the unnamed woman in Mark 14 and Matthew 26 to anoint Jesus' head in preparation for burial. Their actions, their mountain of myrrh and aloes, just as clearly demonstrate their love for Jesus and the depth of their devotion to him. Nicodemus, the Pharisee, ends up in John as an exemplary (male!) disciple.

Yet despite Paul, who was a Pharisee and still proud of the fact (see Philippians 3.5), 'good' Pharisees are rare in the Gospels. We have already seen how Luke in his story of the anointing in chapter 7 turns Simon the Pharisee's offer of hospitality into hostility and insult, and things are no better in 14.1–6, when a leader of the Pharisees invites him to another meal. 'They were watching him closely,' Luke tells us (14.1b). If we wish to grasp the hostility contained in that phrase, we only have to look back just over two chapters to 11.53–54, where 'the scribes and the Pharisees' lie in wait for Jesus, hoping to catch him out in something he might say. Generally speaking, scribes and Pharisees are presented in the Gospels as hostile to Jesus, self-righteous and uncaring, their heads stuck in the sand of a nit-picking preoccupation with the Jewish law, unable to see the truth that stands in Galilean dress in front of them. And that is to demonize them and can never be defended, however hostile *some individuals* may truly have been.

Jesus' teaching and practice were bound to provoke and even antagonize some of his contemporaries. Almost certainly, however, the hostility we find in the Gospels towards the Pharisees and scribes (and 'the Jews' in John) owes more to tensions within Judaism at the time they were written, tensions, that is, between those Jews who accepted Christ and those who found him a *scandalon*, to use Paul's famous term in 1 Corinthians 1.23, a 'scandal' or a 'stumbling-block'.

So when Luke begins his chapter 15 with the 'grumbling' of the scribes and Pharisees, we must beware of taking his words at face value, and we must remain highly suspicious of them when we come to the Parable of the Two Brothers itself. And we must avoid assuming from the start that the parable is going to be all about 'welcoming sinners and eating with them'.

A lost sheep and a lost coin

Before The Two Brothers begins there are two other much smaller parables, The Lost Sheep and The Lost Coin. These are clearly a pair, and Luke presents them as the warm-up act, preparing us for the main event. Some commentators pay sufficient heed to Luke's ordering of things to call The Two Brothers 'The Lost Son'.[10] We do not have the space, alas, to discuss The Lost Sheep and The Lost Coin here. Yet two points do need to be made.

First, they prepare us for some playfulness, or the possibility of it. In The Lost Sheep, for example, the shepherd who has 100 sheep and loses one of them (pretty clever of him to notice that one is missing in a flock that size!) leaves 'the ninety-nine in the wilderness' and goes after the one that is lost (Luke 15.4). As Levine comments, 'The seeker who leaves ninety-nine sheep to find one will have, at the end of the day, only one sheep.'[11] That does not suggest, of course, that Jesus was stupid or knew nothing about shepherding. It simply means he had a lively sense of humour. We may not find ourselves laughing at any point when we come to The Two Brothers, but when we come to its ending we will indeed find plenty of mischief on Jesus' part.

Luke uses The Lost Sheep and The Lost Coin to add to what he thinks The Two Brothers is about. This is our second and more important point. He has Jesus conclude The Lost Coin with the words, 'Just so, I tell you, there is joy in the presence of the angels of God over one sinner who repents' (15.10), and The Lost Sheep with the slightly more elaborate, 'Just so, I tell you, there will be more joy in heaven over one sinner who repents than over ninety-nine righteous persons who need no repentance' (15.7). These words surely do not come from Jesus himself, but from subsequent performers of these parables, whether Luke or those before him who tried to interpret them for their listeners. Whoever they were, they did not do a very good job! Neither the sheep nor the coin is a sinner, nor do they repent. The interpretations do not fit the stories. And who, we might ask, are the 99 righteous persons *who need no repentance*? The Bible, whether Jesus' own Hebrew Scriptures or the New Testament written in his wake (except, it seems for Luke 15.7), is not aware of a single such person, let alone 99 of them out of 100! It is both consistent and insistent in declaring that each and every human being is in need of repentance. This is not playfulness we are dealing with here. It is simply wrong. As it turns out, The Two Brothers will talk of joy and rejoicing (as do The Lost Sheep and The Lost Coin), and there will be repentance also (though some would disagree), but the parable will concern itself with so much else, and if we allow Luke's unlikely comments in 15.7 and 15.10 to direct our reading of it, then we will risk missing all that and, most seriously of all, we will fail to notice the punchline.

The Two Brothers, Act 1, Scene 1: Home: father and son

The parable begins with what is the shortest scene:

> There was a man who had two sons. The younger of them said to his
> father, 'Father, give me the share of the property that will belong to me.'
> So he divided his property between them. (Luke 15.11–12)

'There was a man who had two sons.' No mother then, nor any sisters.
The Lost Coin has just taken us into a woman's world, and, if the
shepherd in The Lost Sheep gives us a picture of God, as so many
argue it does, then the woman desperately searching for the drachma
she has lost, finding it and then laying on a party for the whole village
(costing, no doubt, far more than a drachma!), she too presents us
with an image of God to hold in the soul. But in The Two Brothers
there are no women to be seen. There is, of course, nothing to stop us
imagining them, but there are two particular reasons for their being
kept out of sight. The cast of any of Jesus' parables is very small. There
may be a crowd of extras, such as 'the friends and neighbours' in The
Lost Sheep or The Lost Coin, or indeed the other sheep and coins, but
the main characters are always very few. Otherwise the parable will
not work. In The Lost Sheep or The Lost Coin there are just two (if
we count the sheep or coin that is lost and then found); in The Two
Brothers there will be three, plus a young slave who will have a part
to play in one of the scenes. Second, and more importantly perhaps,
Jesus is tapping here into a rich vein of stories about fathers and sons
and stories of sibling rivalry.

Should we hold some of those prior stories in our minds as we
go through this parable, and if so, which ones? Kenneth Bailey is the
author of a book of over 200 pages entitled *Jacob and the Prodigal:
How Jesus Retold Israel's Story*,[12] and his title makes plain the direction he takes. He argues that we can only get under the skin of the
parable if we look back to the stories in Genesis of fathers who have
two sons, and in particular the story of Isaac and his sons Esau and
Jacob. Snodgrass is dismissive of such a claim, saying that stories of
fathers with two sons were extremely common. The Genesis stories
provide, he says, no more than 'the background music for interpreting
the parable'; they do not hold the key.[13] We need to bear in mind that
Jesus was a rabbi. He may not have had the formal training of a scribe,
but he was regarded as a rabbi and called that by people both within

and outside his circle. Furthermore, the Gospels often speak of him preaching or teaching in synagogues and in the context of synagogue worship. (None of this should surprise us, of course.) It is perfectly reasonable to suppose he performed The Two Brothers at least once in the course of a service in a synagogue, though that can be no more than conjecture, since it does not accord with Luke's setting. Whether in a synagogue or out of it, Jesus would invariably have been addressing religious, observant Jews. He and his contemporaries in Palestine did not live in an age of aggressive secularism, as we now do in this country. His audience, whether in synagogue or out of it, but especially in the context of gathered worship, would have looked to him to throw fresh light on their Scriptures, especially the Torah, of which Genesis is a part. The teaching of his that has come down to us in the Gospels confirms that that was indeed his intention. So we are encouraged to think Bailey might be nearer the truth here than Snodgrass. The questions that remain for us are these: if we look back to those stories of fathers and sons in Genesis, do they help us get into the parable, or do they simply complicate matters? Does the parable enthral us, excite us, surprise, challenge and provoke us, and work for change within us more easily if we hold the Genesis stories in our minds, or if we ignore them? Does the parable take us deeper into the kingdom of God if we hold the hand of the Genesis stories, or do they distract us? The proof of the pudding is in the eating. We can only see what happens when we take certain details of the Genesis stories into account.

'There was a man who had two sons.' That might remind us of Adam and Cain and Abel, of Abraham and his sons Ishmael and Isaac, or Isaac as father of Esau and Jacob. Jonathan Sacks describes sibling rivalry as 'the dominant theme of the book of Genesis'. 'The point could not be made more forcefully,' he continues. '*The first religious act, Cain and Abel's offerings to God, leads directly to the first murder*' (his italics). The Hebrew Bible understands, he says, with Freud and Girard, that 'sibling rivalry is the most primal form of violence'.[14]

But there is no sibling rivalry in The Two Brothers, not yet at least. In Genesis 25 and 27 it is there in full measure. Rebekah, Isaac's wife, gives birth to twin boys, Esau and Jacob. Grown to manhood, Jacob, the younger twin, wants the status, the power, authority and prosperity that belong to his brother. In a nasty little story in Genesis 25.29–34, quite unlike what is to come in this brilliant narrative, he tricks a stupid Esau out of his birthright with no more than a bowl of lentil stew, and with Isaac nowhere to be seen. But things are not that simple. Isaac must make sure the privileges of the elder son are properly passed on to Esau by giving him a deathbed blessing. When Esau is out hunting, Rebekah hatches a plot. With her considerable help Jacob impersonates his brother and succeeds in duping his father. One trick Rebekah uses is to dress him up in Esau's clothes, the finest she has in the house. The frail, blind, dying Isaac gives him his blessing, the blessing he means for Esau, one that includes the lines:

> May God give you of the dew of heaven,
>   and of the fatness of the earth . . .
> Let peoples serve you,
>   and nations bow down to you.
> Be lord over your brothers,
>   and may your mother's sons bow down to you.
>   (Genesis 27.28, 29)

Scarcely has Jacob left his father's presence than Esau enters with a meal he has prepared for his father, a meal which is an important part of the blessing ritual, and which Isaac has already received from Jacob and just eaten. 'Who are you?' Isaac asks him. 'I am your firstborn son, Esau,' he replies. The truth is out! The scene is one of the most poignant in all Scripture and the narrator goes out of his way to help us feel Isaac's and Esau's great distress. He writes with superb skill, and there is no doubt where our sympathies are drawn to lie. Isaac has blessed the wrong son, and he cannot take back his words. 'Bless me, me also, father!' Esau cries, weeping. Isaac does so, but his words only underline the cruelty for both of them of Jacob's deception:

> See, away from the fatness of the earth shall your home be,
>   and away from the dew of heaven on high.
> By your sword you shall live,
>   and you shall serve your brother.   (27.39–40)

We will have to return to other details of this scene in due course, but already, if we hold them in our minds as we turn to the parable, they help underline how much the younger son in the parable humiliates his father in this first scene, and make us wonder at his father's acquiescence.

The scene in the parable is extremely sparse. It has none of the pathos of Genesis 27, not on its surface at least. The younger son's words are so brazen, so blunt they are more command than request: 'Father, give me the share of the property that will belong to me', or, as Joseph Fitmyer translates, 'Father, give me that portion of the property which is coming to me.'[15] (However we translate them, the words in the Greek are just as abrupt.) There is no courtesy here, no shame, no heeding his father's authority, no thought for his feelings. Fathers, and mothers too, of course, still spend time teaching very young children not to talk to them like that. There is no extravagant plotting or preparation, either. This younger son does not need his mother to help him. He enters the stage and comes straight out with it. Though Jesus does not tug at our heartstrings like the writer in Genesis 27, he means us to be shocked here. 'Honour your father and your mother' (Exodus 20.12; Deuteronomy 5.16). So says one of the Ten Commandments from the heart of the Torah – a basic principle of Jewish living. There is no honouring here. The son is thinking of no one but himself, and treats his father with seeming contempt. Snodgrass neatly sums it up: 'He wanted the father's money, not the father.'[16]

'So he divided his property between them.' 'Between *them*.' This would seem to bring the elder son into the picture, but he does not appear. For the moment the parable is only concerned with the father and the younger son. The NRSV's translation 'his property' does not capture the impact of the Greek. There are two different words used in the Greek for 'property' in this verse, and they should not be translated the same. When the son demands his inheritance, he speaks of his share of the *ousia*. The second time, however, the narrator uses the term *bios*, and a more literal and powerful translation of the conclusion to the verse would read, 'So he divided his *life* between them.' That single word, *bios*, hints at what is at stake here, and reminds us that Isaac was on his deathbed when he blessed his sons.

This father is not dying, but for the moment it is as if he was. It was not unheard of in Jewish society for a father to distribute his property to his sons some time before he took to his deathbed, but that was regarded as a very foolish thing to do. Yet in one respect the father does not make a fool of himself. This is not his idea. The younger son tells him to do it. It is the son who makes a fool out of him, and in this significant respect we are very close to Genesis 27.

'So he divided his life between them.' Just like that! No questions, no protest, let alone angry refusal. Eyebrows must surely have shot up at this point in Jesus' audiences, and mouths dropped open. Yet sometimes this is how biblical narrative is. In perhaps the most striking, indeed shocking, example of all, Abraham, when commanded by God to take his son Isaac to the land of Moriah and offer him up as a burnt offering, simply

> rose early in the morning, saddled his donkey, and took two of his young men with him, and his son Isaac . . . cut the wood for the burnt offering, and set out and went to the place in the distance that God had shown him.   (Genesis 22.3)

It is a deliberate narrative technique. The writer of that passage knew what he was doing, and so does Jesus in the parable. And he leaves a vital question hanging in the air: does this father have a favourite son? Rebekah, the mother of the twins, does in Genesis 27, and he too is the younger one, while Jacob himself does ten chapters later: 'Now Israel' (that becomes his new name when he wrestles with God at the Jabbok – see Genesis 32.28) 'loved Joseph more than any other of his children' (Genesis 37.3). Joseph is one of 12 sons, and next to youngest. In the parable, is the father's astonishing and unhesitating acquiescence a sign of favouritism? We shall see.

Act 1, Scene 2: Far from home: the younger son

A few days later the younger son gathered all he had and travelled to a distant country, and there he squandered his property in dissolute living. When he had spent everything, a severe famine took place throughout that country, and he began to be in need. So he went and hired himself out to one of the citizens of that country, who sent him to his fields to feed the pigs. He would gladly have filled himself with the pods that the pigs were eating; and no one gave him anything. But when he came to himself, he said, 'How many of my father's hired hands have bread enough and to spare, but here I am dying of hunger! I will get up and go to my father, and I will say to him, "Father, I have sinned against heaven and before you; I am no longer worthy to be called your son; treat me like one of your hired hands."'   (Luke 15.13–19)

Outrage is piled on outrage! Not only does the son demand his inheritance, but he sells up and goes away to a foreign country and there squanders the lot. 'Honour your father and your mother.' That included caring for them in their old age. He has cast to the winds all his obligations towards them and his responsibilities in the family. He takes himself off, and then in squandering all he has, he loses the material means he might use to care for them. If he does go home, he will be able to do nothing for them. When he comes to his senses at the end of this scene, at least he appears to realize that: he will have to go back not as son, but as a hired hand. And yet we will have reason to doubt the sincerity of his words at that point.

If the first scene was so bare, this one is much richer in detail. The son finds himself in a Gentile country. There is a sense in which we should not make too much of that. Levine comments, 'At the time of Jesus, there were probably more Jews living outside Judea and lower Galilee than there were in the Jewish homeland; over a million were in Alexandria in Egypt.'[17] Yet being in Gentile territory and far from home may be fine in good times when you have plenty of money, but when the money is gone and famine comes, then it is a different story. He gets his comeuppance. No longer does he have the protection of his father, his family or the local community. No longer does he live among a people whose Torah bade them care for the alien in their midst: 'The alien who resides with you shall be to you as the citizen among you; you shall love the alien as yourself, for you were aliens in the land of Egypt: I am the Lord your God' (Leviticus 19.34). 'No one gave him anything,' says the parable. That sums it up. And he, a Jew, is feeding pigs. The Jews did not keep pigs and were forbidden to eat them. In the lower Galilee the people kept faithfully to the law. The archaeologists digging there have unearthed no pig bones.[18] In our first chapter, we found a man, a Gentile calling himself Legion, living with pigs among the dead, and we quoted Isaiah. We need to quote him again, going back to lines just two verses earlier. The speaker here is God himself:

> I held out my hands all day long
> to a rebellious people,
> who walk in a way that is not good,
> following their own devices . . .
> who sit inside tombs,
> and spend the night in secret places;
> who eat swine's flesh.
>
> (Isaiah 65.2, 4)

But the son cannot eat the pigs he is hired to feed. He cannot even eat their food. He, a Jew, longs to eat like a pig, but he cannot. He is starving to death in a country in the grip of famine.

There are further echoes of the Genesis stories here. Jacob finds himself in exile for 20 years in the land of Haran. Esau is so angry that his brother has tricked him out of his inheritance that he means to kill him. Rebekah gets to hear of it and tells Jacob to escape there. Yet Haran is not unknown territory. It is where Abraham once came from, and Rebekah herself. She sends Jacob to the protection of her brother Laban. I once wrote:

> Jacob is a trickster . . . Outwitting his brother and father was straight-forward enough. His uncle Laban is a different proposition altogether. He is a trickster too. The presence of two tricksters on stage at one and the same time is bound to make for comedy, and so it does here. At one or two points the Jacob/Laban stories approach bedroom farce. Jacob learns what it feels like to be cheated himself, even on a wedding night for which he has waited seven years! Laban puts the wrong daughter of his in Jacob's bed, and Jacob does not realize it till he wakes up in the morning![19]

There is no comedy in the second scene of The Two Brothers, no farce. And the son will return home with nothing. Jacob eventually returns with 2 wives, 11 sons and a daughter, male and female slaves, and with large flocks and herds. Oh, and with Laban's household gods stolen by one of his wives!

The situation of the son in the parable is closer in some respects to that of Joseph in the later chapters of Genesis. His elder brothers are understandably jealous of him, because their father so clearly loves him more than them, and because he will keep having dreams about them bowing down to him and then take the trouble to tell them all about them. Seething with anger they plot to kill him, but they end up selling him into slavery in Egypt. He is sold to a high-ranking Egyptian called Potiphar, but when Potiphar's wife falsely accuses him of trying to rape her, he finds himself in prison. From a dungeon where he could be expected to see out his days he makes an astonishing rise to power, until the Pharaoh appoints him his second-in-command. 'See, I have set you over all the land of Egypt,' he says to him. 'Removing his signet ring from his hand, Pharaoh put it on Joseph's hand; he arrayed him in garments of fine linen, and put a gold chain round his neck' (Genesis 41.41b–42). Egypt is plunged into seven years of famine, but Joseph has predicted them and in seven years of particularly abundant harvests has built and filled enough storehouses to save the whole people from starvation (see Genesis 41.46–57).

We will soon have cause to return to these passages, but for now we can only see how far away the son in the parable is from Joseph when famine arrives at his door. To be precise, he does not even have a door. He is out in the open with the pigs, as they gorge themselves on their carob pods. He will have no miraculous rise to power here. His only hope is to return home. He will surely not be able to rise to power there, either. He will have to live as a hired hand, getting work from his father when he can. Or perhaps . . .

How do we hear the words he plans to say when he reaches his father? There are no instructions in the text about how they should be read, about the tone of voice the reader should employ. Encouraged by Luke's reference to repentance at the close of The Lost Sheep, and again at the end of The Lost Coin, many have heard the son's speech as one of genuine remorse. He certainly speaks the truth. He has indeed wronged both God and his father, and grievously so; he deserves to be disowned by his father. But why then does he mean to address him as 'father'? In the next scene of the parable we will have to spend some time looking at the brilliant, heartwarming, heartrending Genesis

33 and its story of Jacob's reunion with his brother. Returning from Haran, Jacob sends messengers to his brother and carefully instructs them what to say:

> Thus you shall say to my lord Esau: Thus says your servant Jacob, 'I have lived with Laban as an alien, and stayed until now; and I have donkeys, flocks, male and female slaves; and I have sent to tell my lord, in order that I may find favour in your sight.' (Genesis 32.4–5)

Hearing that Esau is coming to meet him with what sounds like a small army of 400 men, he prays to God:

> I am not worthy of the least of all the steadfast love and all the faithfulness that you have shown to your servant . . . Deliver me, please, from the hand of my brother, from the hand of Esau, for I am afraid of him; he may come and kill us all, the mothers with the children. (Genesis 32.10, 11)

He sends fine gifts ahead of him: 'For he thought, "I may appease him with the present that goes ahead of me, and afterwards I shall see his face; perhaps he will accept me" ' (32.20). When eventually he meets his brother, he does not dare look him in the face but bows himself to the ground seven times. The gifts have together amounted to 550 animals. Again I wrote:

> They are gifts fit for a king, and so they are meant to be. Jacob cannot approach Esau as a brother. He can only approach him as a vassal might approach a great overlord, a rebellious vassal at that, who now repents his treachery and wishes to make amends.[20]

Returning to the parable from Genesis 32 and 33, we are struck immediately by the familiarity of the son's address to his father. He will not be bowing himself to the ground seven times, that is for sure. Yes, Jacob hopes against hope that his gifts and his words will win round his brother, and they are carefully designed to do just that. Yet there is a genuine remorse about them, as his prayer to God underlines. When he meets his brother he gives him back the blessing he has stolen from him.[21] No further proof is needed of his repentance, and Esau takes the gift, accepts it as gift, no longer his right. It is one of the great moments in all Scripture. The son's speech in The Two Brothers contains no repentance, none at least that I can hear.

It is not insignificant that the son begins by reflecting upon his own situation: 'How many of my father's hired hands have bread enough and to spare, but here I am dying of hunger!' *That* is why he is going back, not because he is full of remorse for what he has done but because he wishes to survive. He hopes against hope to win his father round, hence his talk of sin and unworthiness. He tries to make it easier for his father by suggesting he treat him like a hired hand. But he is hoping for more than that. Despite what he says, he is hoping, perhaps even expecting, to be taken back as son. That is why he plans to call him 'father'. That single word undermines the rest. Will the father see through it, as we have?

Act 1, Scene 3: Returning home: son and father

So he set off and went to his father. But while he was still far off, his father saw him and was filled with compassion; he ran and put his arms around him and kissed him. Then the son said to him, 'Father, I have sinned against heaven and before you; I am no longer worthy to be called your son.' But the father said to his slaves, 'Quickly, bring out a robe – the best one – and put it on him; put a ring on his finger and sandals on his feet. And get the fatted calf and kill it, and let us eat and celebrate; for this son of mine was dead and is alive again; he was lost and is found!' And they began to celebrate. (Luke 15.20–24)

We know this story too well, and this scene is its most famous. Let us try to hear it as if for the first time, for only then can we catch its surprise and perceive its shadows.

No time is spent on the son's long journey home, not until he gets within sight of his village. Or, to be more precise, within his father's sight. It is as if his father has been watching for him all this time, his eyes fixed on that point on his horizon where the track disappears, the track his son took when he left home. His eyes are still sharp. He sees him, he recognizes him, he can see the state of him. And so he runs. 'I held out my hands all day long to a rebellious people,' says the God of Isaiah. The prophet's imagery is exquisite. But the father of Jesus' parable goes beyond it. He *runs*. He runs because he is filled with compassion. Biblical stories often leave people's motives unstated. Not here. And before his son can say anything he falls upon his neck (a more literal translation of the Greek) and kisses him. When Joseph in Genesis is reunited with Benjamin and his other brothers, he and Benjamin fall upon each other's neck and weep, and then Joseph kisses all his brothers and weeps upon them, too (Genesis 45.14–15). When in Acts Paul bids farewell to the elders of the church at Ephesus, and tells them they will not see him again, they fall on his neck and kiss him (Acts 20.37 – Luke there uses exactly the same Greek verbs as he does in The Two Brothers). But in one other passage in Scripture, and only one, a person *runs* to meet someone, and then falls on his neck and kisses him, and that person is Esau in Genesis 33.4, when he is reunited with his brother.

Jacob has been afraid that Esau is coming to kill him. We have been sharing his fear, we, the readers and hearers of the story, for we too have heard nothing of Esau since the time when he was planning

105

to kill his brother. His greeting Jacob so warmly, his forgiving him, and the magnanimity he displays throughout the passage, are totally unexpected. Suddenly he emerges as one of the great heroes of biblical narrative. He cares nothing about the past, the great wrong that Jacob did to him and to their father, the unbearable hurt it caused. His brother is back, and that fills his world. It is all he cares about. They are reunited, and it is all that matters.

The way the father in the parable runs to greet his son is also unexpected. The son fears being disowned by him. That is clear from the speech he has prepared. We, perhaps, have not known quite what to expect, but surely not *this*, this running, this warm embrace, this kissing over and over. The Greek verb for 'kissed him' is a strong one, and we have, in fact, come across it before: Luke uses it twice in the story of the woman who kisses and anoints Jesus' feet in the house of Simon the Pharisee, in 7.38 and 45. The Greek of verse 45 is especially instructive. Jesus says to Simon, 'You gave me no kiss, but from the time I came in she has not stopped kissing my feet.' The first word for 'kiss' there is *philema*, the second for 'kissing' is *kataphilousa*. *Philema* is a formal kiss of welcome (which, of course, is all Jesus would have expected). *Kataphilousa* suggests a greater depth of feeling. *Kataphilousa* suggests love.

And we cannot emphasize enough that the father's greeting comes *before* the son utters his speech. His son is back, and that fills his world. They are reunited, and that is all that matters. 'This son of mine was dead and is alive again,' he cries to the slaves; 'he was lost and is found!' And of course, his son is in a much worse state than Jacob is in Genesis 33. Jacob returns from Haran a wealthy man. The son is destitute and starving. He is as Rembrandt portrays him in that great masterpiece in the Hermitage in St Petersburg. So the father's receiving him back is filled with compassion also, as we are told. And there is no time to be lost. His son needs to be clothed and shod and fed, and quickly. Forgiveness comes before any repentance here, as so often it does with Jesus in the Gospels. We are told time and again that we must repent in order to be forgiven. Not so in the parable. It is the other way round. Forgiveness creates repentance. For *after* the father's greeting, *then* the son says, 'Father, I have sinned against heaven and before you; I am no longer worthy to be called your son,' and this time he means it.

Not everyone would agree with that judgement. Levine remains suspicious of the son, and is still disconcerted by his addressing his father as 'Father', rather than 'Sir', or 'Lord' or 'Master'.[22] Yet what else can he call the man who has just run up the road to meet him? How else can he respond to that act of love and compassion? He has been received back as *son*, and with an affection beyond his wildest dreams. To call him anything but 'Father' in return would almost amount to an insult, at least to a refusal to share his love and accept his forgiveness. This time calling him 'Father' does not represent an attempt to manipulate, but shows that his love is received, felt, reciprocated.

His father's welcome also explains why his speech is shorter this time. It is exactly the same as the one he rehearsed, until he gets towards the end. This time he says nothing about being treated like one of his father's hired hands. How can he, when his father has run to greet him as a long-lost son?

So now the son has not simply come to himself, as the parable puts it in verse 17, but has arrived at true repentance. He has returned to love, to his father's love for him and to his own love for his father. It is a true homecoming, as Rembrandt so wonderfully portrays.

And it would indeed be wonderful, and all would be well and all manner of things would be well, if this was the father's only son. But he is not. We have so wanted a happy ending that we have put the elder son quite out of our minds (after all, where has he been in the story thus far?) and effectively ended the story there. We have called it the Parable of the Prodigal Son, and ignored the rest. Yet it begins, 'There was a man who had *two* sons.' Suppose it began, 'There was a man who had a son', and their reunion marked its ending, why then it would be quite a different parable.

If we remember the other son, suddenly the father's welcome of this younger son and the way it is described make us uneasy. The sandals for his feet are relatively innocent. They make clear to all that he is not a slave and cannot be ordered around like the slaves who are told to fetch them. The robe and the ring, however, are another matter. The ring recalls the one that Pharaoh puts on Joseph's finger when he appoints him his second-in-command. 'You shall be over my house,' he tells him, 'and all my people shall order themselves as you command' (Genesis 41.40). And the robe for the son reminds us of the 'garments of fine linen' in the same passage in which Pharaoh dresses him for his new position of authority (41.42). That is power dressing, pure and simple. Where, we wonder, does it leave the elder brother in the parable?

Our unease is sharpened by other memories, of Joseph's 'coat of many colours', as it has been called, or 'richly embroidered tunic', as perhaps the Hebrew of Genesis 37.3 should be translated, the one that he is famously given by his father. That verse in Genesis reads, 'Now Israel' (that is Jacob) 'loved Joseph more than any other of his children . . . and he made him a richly embroidered tunic.'[23] Joseph's coat is thus a sign of Jacob's favouritism, one that cannot be missed, a constant reminder to his older brothers of where they stand, or do not stand, in their father's affections.

And there is a third cross-reference we can make, perhaps the most disturbing of all: to Rebekah's dressing Jacob in Esau's clothes before he enters Isaac's presence to receive his blessing. 'Then Rebekah took the best garments of her elder son Esau, which were with her in the house, and put them on her younger son Jacob' (Genesis 27.15). When the father in the parable calls for the best robe in the house to be fetched, is it the one that rightfully belongs to the elder brother, and is it a sign for all to see that *this* son, this one, is his favourite? If Luke's Greek is translated more literally, the father says to the slaves, 'Quickly, bring out a robe – the *first* one.' So does it put the son who wears it first, *ahead of his brother*?

The feast begins, no doubt with all the father's friends and neighbours present,[24] and with the younger son in the place of honour.

It is time for the spotlight to swing round, for the elder brother to appear. It is time for the second act to start.

Act 2, Scene 1: Outside: the elder son

Now his elder son was in the field; and when he came and approached the house, he heard music and dancing. He called one of the slaves and asked what was going on. He replied, 'Your brother has come, and your father has killed the fatted calf, because he has got him back safe and sound.' Then he became angry and refused to go in. (Luke 15.25–28a)

Every word counts. The elder son 'was in the field'. That might sound innocent enough and of little consequence, but for us with an ear for the Genesis stories it reminds us of Esau. In Genesis 27.3 Isaac says to him, 'Now then, take your weapons, your quiver and your bow, and *go out to the field*, and hunt game for me.' In the field is precisely where Esau is when his brother goes into his father's presence and steals his blessing. And he returns from there to discover to his great horror what has happened.

'In the field' suggests distance, remoteness, aloneness. In the parable everyone seems to have heard about his brother's return apart from the elder son. Their bellies full of fatted calf and drink, they are now making merry with music and dancing. They have started without him. His father has started without him. He has to learn about it all from a slave-boy (the Greek word used is *pais*, not the usual *doulos*, suggesting someone young). The boy does not mention the running up the track, the sandals, the ring or that 'first' robe. He does not need to. His mention of the killing of the fatted calf and the sounds of celebrating are enough. We have to imagine a society in which families did not often have meat to eat, and a fatted calf is the very best any of them could look forward to, a beast whose slaughter is kept for very special occasions. The elder son has heard enough to know what is going on, and it is enough to release his anger.

The slave-boy speaks of 'your brother'. He introduces into the parable the word 'brother' (we have not heard it before this), and thereby he brings to its surface the theme of sibling rivalry. It was anticipated at the very start, with the opening words, 'There was a man who had two sons.' Its shadow made us uneasy when we explored the welcome the father gives to the younger brother. It will now dominate the rest of the parable.

The anger of the elder brother once again makes us think of Esau in Genesis 27. 'Now Esau hated Jacob because of the blessing with which his father had blessed him, and Esau said to himself, "The days of mourning for my father are approaching; then I will kill my brother Jacob" ' (Genesis 27.41). But Esau does not hate his father, for he knows he was tricked into doing what he did. The slave-boy explains, however, that the father of the parable has organized a feast for his younger son 'because he has got him back safe and sound'. That makes it worse for this elder brother. For now he has his proof: his father has a favourite, and it is not him. He is left more isolated than Esau, for Esau did not lose his father or his father's affection. The elder son of the parable has lost both his brother and his father. And no mother, no sisters are mentioned anywhere. So he has lost everything. He is utterly alone, an outsider for whom there can be no homecoming, for who will kill the fatted calf for *him*? He refuses to join the feast. His duty as elder son is to help his father entertain the guests. His father has welcomed his brother back with joy, because he is safe and sound. He must do the same, even if he has to grit his teeth and pretend his joy. The feast is an event of huge significance for the family and the community. But his hurt is too sharp. The feast is not for him. He refuses to go in.

There is tragedy here. Or so it *seems*.

Act 2, Scene 2: Outside: father and son

His father came out and began to plead with him. But he answered his father, 'Listen! For all these years I have been working like a slave for you, and I have never disobeyed your command; yet you have never given me even a young goat so that I might celebrate with my friends. But when this son of yours came back, who has devoured your property with prostitutes, you killed the fatted calf for him!' Then the father said to him, 'Dear child, you are always with me, and all that is mine is yours.'

(Luke 15.28b–31. The NRSV has 'Son' in that last verse; we will explain our translation 'Dear child' in due course.)

Scene 1 runs straight into Scene 2. Indeed, in the Greek this final scene begins halfway through a sentence. There is no change of place, and the elder son does not need to move. But there is a journey. The father leaves his place at the feast, leaves behind the dance and comes to the outside, to the place where his son is. He could have sent a slave to call his son inside. He could have sent to remind the son in no uncertain terms of his duty. He could have issued a command. Instead he comes out to beg him, to plead with him. Elsewhere in his Gospel Luke uses the same Greek verb, *parakalein*, when Legion's demons *beg* Jesus not to send them into the abyss (8.31), and again when Jairus falls at Jesus' feet and *begs* him to come and heal his daughter when she is at the point of death (8.41). It is a strong word. The father's journey to his elder son is not so dramatic as when he runs up the track to welcome home his younger son, but it is every bit as significant. In neither scene has the father the slightest concern for his authority within the family, his honour, dignity or pride, or his standing in the community. He just wishes to reach his son, first the younger, then the elder. His running up the track is an act of love and compassion. So is his coming out of the feast.

He is met this time with fury and raw pain. His elder son does not entirely tell the truth. He says he has been 'slaving' for his father for so many years (the Greek is sharper and more concise than 'working like a slave'), but slaves do not, cannot talk to their masters like this. We might say that sons do not talk to their fathers like this, either, but we need to recall how God himself is sometimes addressed in the Hebrew Scriptures. In Exodus 5.22–23 Moses turns to God and says,

My lord, why have you brought disaster to this people? Why the hell did you send me? Ever since I came to Pharaoh to speak in your name,

111

he has brought disaster to this people! And as for rescuing, you have not rescued your people!'[25]

In *Face to Face with God* I commented on this prayer and described God as being 'under verbal attack'. 'Moses' words are savage with anger,' I continued.

> He makes a direct comparison between God and Pharaoh, and a devastating one it is: they have brought nothing but disaster to his people; God also is the enemy; he is another thug, and the Israelites are victims of his brutality also.[26]

Moses there does not speak the truth, either, for God is not the enemy of his people, and is far from being a brutal thug like Pharaoh. Yet Moses prays as he feels and, driven by a sense of powerlessness, prays as he hurts. The elder son does the same, and if Moses can speak to God like that, then he can address his father like this. His outburst does not begin with 'My lord', or even 'Father'. It lacks all courtesy. At the same time his accusation is not nearly as serious as the one Moses makes against God.

Has he really been nursing such resentment 'all these years', or has his fury led him to exaggerate that, too? It is possible he has had his suspicions about his father's feelings for his brother ever since he gave in so easily to that curt demand for his inheritance. The elder son has been there all the time in this story. It is just that we have not heard or seen him before.

His words would seem at first to isolate him from his father. They certainly declare his distance from his brother. 'This son of yours', he calls him. He cannot even bear to say the words, 'my brother'. And when he speaks of him having 'devoured your *property*', he uses the same word, *bios*, as we heard at the beginning of the story. 'He has eaten up your life' is a more literal translation of what he tells his father. 'He has eaten up your life *with prostitutes*.' How does he know that? He may be right, of course. We were told in Act 1, Scene 2, that the younger son 'squandered his property' (*ousia*) 'in dissolute living'. Yet there was no communication between him and the family, as far as we know, not until he came home with nothing. The elder son is not relying on his own special knowledge. It is his jealousy speaking, and a burning desire to put his brother in as bad a light as possible with his father. It is a protest, as indeed is his whole speech, against what he perceives as his father's favouritism. 'You have never given me so much as a young goat! But it's the fatted calf for him!'

His speech has the plain-speaking of a Moses, but chiefly it reminds us of Jacob in Genesis 31, when he lays into his uncle Laban.

> These twenty years I have been with you; your ewes and your female goats have not miscarried, and I have not eaten the rams of your flocks. That which was torn by wild beasts I did not bring to you; I bore the loss of it myself; of my hand you required it, whether stolen by day or stolen by night. It was like this with me: by day the heat consumed me, and the cold by night, and my sleep fled from my eyes. These twenty years I have been in your house; I served you [we could translate, 'I slaved for you'] fourteen years for your two daughters, and six years for your flock, and you have changed my wages ten times. (31.38–41)

Despite the differences in the detail the echoes of this speech in the parable are clear. But why should Jesus take us back *there*, to Jacob's complaints against his uncle?[27] The answer lies in Laban's answer: 'The daughters are my daughters, the children are my children, the flocks are my flocks, *and all that you see is mine*' (31.43).

The father in The Two Brothers calls his elder son, 'Dear child'. The NRSV has 'Son'. That catches the terseness of the Greek, which has but a single word, *teknon*. But *teknon* means 'child'. The word used so often in this parable for son is *huios*. *Teknon* is a more affectionate term. 'Dear child' conveys the sense. Scott observes that the Greek of the rest of the father's response is in carefully balanced, rhythmic speech,[28] and that serves to emphasize its importance. The rhythms add to its sonority.

'*Dear child, you are always with me, and all that is mine is yours.*' *That* is the punchline! It changes everything. It is, of course, the opposite of what Laban says to Jacob, and the contrast makes us sit up and take notice.

The writer of the story of Jonah uses a similar narrative device. His tale is hilarious, with a pantomime prophet, a pantomime storm, a pantomime fish, a pantomime king with pantomime people and animals, a pantomime plant and even, until the very end, a pantomime God. And then, in the last verse, he turns everything upside down. 'Go at once to Nineveh,' God tells Jonah at the start of the story, 'that great city, and cry against it; for their wickedness has come up before me' (Jonah 1.2). Jonah's story was probably written at a time of crisis, when the great enemy was no longer Assyria, with its capital of Nineveh, but Babylon or Persia. Yet the memory of the Assyrians, their ruthlessness and brutal conquest of the kingdoms of Israel and Judah, was still strong, just as the memory of Hitler's Third Reich will continue to play its part in the Jewish consciousness for very many years to come. When Jonah eventually reaches Nineveh, he denounces it: 'Forty days more, and Nineveh will be overthrown.' And instantly the king, his nobles, his people and even their animals repent! It is impossible, of course . . . and it drives Jonah wild! Then, at the very end, after more fun and games with a plant that springs up to shade Jonah from the heat and just as quickly withers and dies, God asks Jonah a question: *'Should I not pity Nineveh?'* With that the story comes to an abrupt end. We are not told Jonah's response, and that is because the storyteller wants *us* to answer it. The question is left hanging in the air, a question asked by God himself, who has put off his pantomime costume and revealed his universal, astonishing compassion. It is one of the great questions in the Bible, as important now as it was then. In the silence that followed it the first hearers of the story suddenly found they had to answer it, and ever since all readers and hearers of the story have had to make their response, substituting for Nineveh their own centre of oppression.

Now that we have reached the end of the Parable of the Two Brothers we see Jesus also has been playing with us. From the start he has convinced us the father of his story is a fool. He has led us to suspect he has a favourite son, and in the middle of the story that seems all too plain. Thanks to the welcome he receives, and that robe, ring and feast, the younger son, against all deserving, appears to be paraded before the family and the village as the one his father loves. He is the heir now. To all intents and purposes he is the elder son. If you doubt that, just look at him! Jesus has led us a long way up the garden path, for the father saying to the true elder son, 'Dear child, you are always with me, and all that is mine is yours', unravels all we thought we knew. 'Dear child', that one Greek word *teknon*, means the father does not have favourites after all; he loves both his sons equally. (His leaving the feast to plead with his elder son has already suggested that is the case.) 'You are always with me' – the elder son is not the outsider he thought he was. 'All that is mine is yours' – he remains the heir. And yet the younger son is still in the middle of the feast in his new sandals and richly embroidered tunic, with his father's ring upon his finger. We end up with a gloriously impossible tale of a father with *two elder sons*. It was not what we expected.

We do not hear how the elder son (or should we call him the second of the elder sons?) responds. Does he join the feast? Does he embrace his brother and take his place in the dance? Jesus does not tell us. It is that old storyteller's trick. His silence throws the question at us. Will *we* join the feast? Will *we* embrace our brother and take *our* part in the dance?

In Luke's performance of the parable there are a few words more. The father continues with, 'But we had to celebrate and rejoice, because this brother of yours was dead and has come to life; he was lost and has been found.' The phrase 'this brother of yours' neatly answers the elder son's calling his brother 'this son of yours', but I strongly suspect these lines owe more to Luke than to Jesus.[29] They lessen the impact of the punchline, and risk spoiling it altogether. For they are, of course, a reprise of the end of the father's speech to his slaves at the end of Act 1. They draw our minds back to that moment and focus our attention once more on the younger son. They are a distraction and they let us off the hook, for they leave the matter with this fictional elder son. How will he respond? Jesus was not interested in that. This is a *parable*, not a story told for our amusement, however entertaining it might be along the way. It was meant to enthral those who heard it, inspire them, challenge and change them. It is carefully designed to do the same to us.

For the punchline to have its impact, we need to identify ourselves with the elder son. That itself may come as a surprise, for we have been taught so long to ignore the elder son and identify with the younger one. Yet Jesus' first hearers would surely not have been so sympathetic towards the younger son, given the way he treats his father, and they would have been made uneasy by the extravagance of the father's welcoming him back home. They would have readily understood the elder son's outburst in the second act, and would not have been disconcerted by the way he speaks to his father. 'He had it coming to him,' they would have said. And so they would have fallen straight into Jesus' trap. He would have looked them in the eye. *Would they join the dance of the kingdom of God?* For that is what the celebrations signify.

Narrative and counter-narrative: the challenge of the parable

The narratives in Genesis to which we have so often made reference in this chapter are the stories of the ancestors of the people of Israel, the ancestors of the Jews for whom Jesus performed his parable. They are the strangest, the most wonderful tales of a people's ancestors ever told. They refuse to turn them into heroes. Thinking of the Hebrew Bible as a whole, Jonathan Sacks comments: 'Israel, to a degree unique in history, produced a literature of almost uninterrupted self-criticism.'[30] I used to tell my students, when I was teaching Old Testament Studies at Salisbury and Wells Theological College, 'If you didn't know this stuff was written by Jews, you might think it was anti-Semitic.' Nor do the ancestor stories of Genesis demonize their rivals. Quite the reverse.

The people of Israel declared themselves descended from younger sons: from Isaac, not his older half-brother Ishmael; from Jacob, not Esau. They went on to speak of Joseph as a favoured younger son (the eleventh out of 12) and the ancestor of one of the most important tribes in Israel. Yet we have already seen with Esau how he emerges in Genesis 33 as one of the true heroes of the Bible. His generosity and magnanimity, his forgiveness and greatness of spirit go beyond anything that his brother Jacob anywhere displays. Jacob to his credit, and in a few most extraordinary words, acknowledges that is so: 'truly to see your face is like seeing the face of God' (Genesis 33.10). Jacob knows what he is talking about. He has spent the previous night wrestling with God, and has declared, 'I have seen God face to face' (32.30). Now as he faces his brother, he finds himself looking again into the eyes of God.

The reconciliation of the two brothers in Genesis 33 comes so very close, and that is thanks to Esau. If he were allowed to determine the course of the narrative, then it would be complete. He says to his brother, 'Let us journey on our way, and I will go alongside you' (33.12). Jacob protests weakly that he and his large entourage are too slow to follow at Esau's pace. Esau is on his way back to Seir to the south of the Dead Sea. 'I will lead on slowly,' says Jacob, 'according to the pace of the cattle that are before me and according to the pace of the children, until I come to my lord in Seir' (33.14b). It is disappointing that Jacob still insists on calling his brother 'my lord'. It goes beyond disappointment that he has no intention of joining him in Seir. As soon as Esau and his men have left, Jacob turns west and heads for the land of Canaan. Why so? Because Esau is destined by God to be the ancestor of a people called the Edomites, while Jacob's descendants will be the people of Israel in the land of Canaan. The moment when Jacob turns west is one of the most tragic in all Scripture, and the narrator has gone out of his way to help us recognize it. It is as if he composes his narrative with heavy reluctance, as if he is protesting against the direction he knows it must follow.

We have seen it before in Genesis. When first he appears in the narrative Abraham receives commands and promises from God: 'Go from your country and your kindred and your father's house to the land that I will show you. I will make of you a great nation, and I will bless you, and make your name great' (Genesis 12.1–2). For those promises to be fulfilled Abraham must have a son (in the world of Genesis a daughter will not do). That son will turn out to be Isaac. But Isaac has an older half-brother, Ishmael, and the narrator calls on all his considerable storytelling powers to draw our sympathies towards him and his mother, Sarah's Egyptian slave-girl, Hagar. Twice Hagar is driven away into the desert, once when she is pregnant with Ishmael and again when he is a small child. These passages, Genesis 16 and 21.8–21, are most poignant ones. We are drawn into recognizing, into feeling Hagar's plight and that of her child. At the same time she is accorded privileges which mark her out and put her on a high pedestal, far above her mistress Sarah, who is painted in these stories as a wholly tragic character.[31] Chapter 16 is Hagar's annunciation scene. She is one of just two women in the Bible to receive an annunciation from God himself (the other is Manoah's wife in Judges 13; Mary of Nazareth encounters an angel); she *sees God*, and so joins another very select body of biblical characters; she gives God a name, and in that respect is unique.[32] Chapter 21 finds her and her young son wandering in the desert of Beer-sheba. Their water runs out and Hagar casts Ishmael in the shade of a bush and sits on the ground to wait for his death, and her own. God again comes to their rescue. In the very next chapter we have the story of the binding of Isaac, when another son comes close to death and is saved by God's intervention. But that is told in an entirely matter-of-fact manner, and is devoid of emotion. Sacks comments on the two passages:

> There is a pathos here [in Genesis 21] that is rare in biblical prose.
> There can be no doubt that the narrative is written to enlist our sym-
> pathy in a way it does not in the case of Isaac. We *identify* with Hagar
> and Ishmael; we are *awed* by Abraham and Isaac.[33]

(Some of us are more horrified than awed.)

Yet it was Isaac, not Ishmael, who was the ancestor of those who
wrote these tales.

There is an ancient narrative, based on a superficial reading of
these texts and popular in the Church from the time of Paul, a powerful one also in Judaism and Islam, of a God who has his favourites,
who faced with two sons of the same father chooses one and rejects
the other. And except in Islam it is the younger of the two who is
the chosen one. It begins as far back as Genesis 4, when God accepts
Abel's offering, but has no regard for the offering of his older brother
Cain (4.3–5). It continues with Ishmael and Isaac, when Abraham
cries out to God, 'O that Ishmael might live in your sight!' and God
replies, 'No, but your wife Sarah will bear you a son, and you shall
name him Isaac. I will establish my covenant with him as an ever-
lasting covenant for his offspring after him' (Genesis 17.18–19).
For Isaac to flourish and to fulfil his divine destiny, Ishmael and his
mother must be banished to the desert and come near to death. As
for Esau and Jacob, we have already seen that it is their God-given
destinies that lead to the parting of their ways. Before they are born
God tells Rebekah:

> Two nations are in your womb,
>   and two peoples born of you shall be divided;
> the one shall be stronger than the other,
>   the elder shall serve the younger.
> (Genesis 25.23)[34]

This narrative, of a God who chooses one and rejects another, is given
a nasty twist elsewhere in the Old Testament. Esau was the ancestor
of the Edomites and for centuries Israel and Edom were sworn enemies. David waged a six-month campaign against them, and much
later, at the beginning of the sixth century BC, when the Babylonians
besieged Jerusalem, the Edomites were their allies. They took part in
the capture and looting of the city, and when so many of the people
of Judah were taken captive to Babylonia , they took advantage of the
vulnerability of those who were left behind, moved into the southern

part of their country and established their own capital in Hebron. In bitter words the prophet Obadiah declares how God will wreak vengeance on Edom, or on Esau, as he also calls the people. 'There shall be no survivor of the house of Esau,' he cries, 'for the LORD has spoken' (Obadiah 18b).[35] Then in the book of the prophet Malachi we find the notorious declaration put into God's mouth: 'I have loved Jacob, but I have hated Esau' (Malachi 1.2–3a). God continues in the next verse,

> If Edom says, 'We are shattered but we will rebuild the ruins,' the LORD of hosts says: They may rebuild, but I will tear down, until they are called the wicked country, the people with whom the LORD is angry for ever.

The invective of Psalm 83 brings Edom and the Ishmaelites together in its list of the enemies of the people of God, and prays that God

> make them like whirling dust,
> like chaff before the wind.
> (Psalm 83.13)

To this Genesis offers a powerful counter-narrative, and it is not the only place in the Old Testament that does so.

> You shall not abhor any of the Edomites, for they are your kin. You shall not abhor any of the Egyptians, because you were an alien residing in their land. The children of the third generation that are born to them may be admitted to the assembly of the Lord. (Deuteronomy 23.7–8).

Amos may not mention either the Edomites or the Ishmaelites, but the words he places in God's mouth go even further than Deuteronomy in their attitude to neighbouring peoples, including ones who had been Israel's enemies:

> Are you not like the Ethiopians to me,
> O people of Israel? says the LORD.
> Did I not bring Israel up from the land of Egypt,
> and the Philistines from Caphtor and the Arameans from Kir?
> (Amos 9.7)

A passage in Isaiah contains a series of sayings about the Egyptians which include the startling words:

> When they cry to the LORD because of oppressors, he will send them a saviour, and will defend and deliver them. The Lord will make himself

known to the Egyptians; and the Egyptians will know the LORD on that day, and will worship with sacrifice and burnt-offering, and they will make vows to the LORD and perform them ... On that day Israel will be the third with Egypt and Assyria, a blessing in the midst of the earth, whom the LORD of hosts has blessed, saying, 'Blessed be Egypt my people, and Assyria the work of my hands, and Israel my heritage.'   (Isaiah 19.20b–21, 24–25)

And then, of course, there is that question at the end of the story of Jonah: 'Should I not pity Nineveh?', as well as the statement in Genesis 1.26–27 that *all* human beings are made in the image and likeness of God, one of the most radical, profound, challenging and hope-creating statements ever made.

Sacks describes Genesis as 'the foundational book of Abrahamic monotheism' and says, 'The conclusion to which the whole of Genesis has been leading is *the rejection of rejection*.'[36] He offers that as a comment on the story of the final reconciliation between Joseph and his brothers. But 'the rejection of rejection' is a fitting title for this whole counter-narrative, where none have to compete for God's favour, for all are cherished, all are loved, all are his children.

In the Parable of the Two Brothers Jesus appears, right until the very end, to be following the other narrative, the one of a father, of a God who chooses one and rejects another, who has a younger son as his favourite. And then, with the words, 'Dear child, you are always with me, and all that is mine is yours', he suddenly reveals he has been deceiving us. The father of the parable, and the rabbi who tells the tale, Jesus of Nazareth, there make their final choice: the counter-narrative. Jesus chooses the rejection of rejection, and challenges his hearers to do the same. Cast as the elder son, now, not the younger, will they join the feast, will they embrace their brother, will they join the dance of the kingdom of God?

> On this mountain the LORD of hosts will make for all peoples
>   a feast of rich food, a feast of well-matured wines,
>   of rich food filled with marrow, of well-matured wines strained
>   clear.
> And he will destroy on this mountain
>   the shroud that is cast over all peoples,
>   the sheet that is spread over all nations;
>   he will swallow up death for ever.
> Then the LORD God will wipe away the tears from all faces,

and the disgrace of his people he will take away from all the earth,
for the LORD has spoken.
It will be said on that day,
Lo, this is our God; we have waited for him, so that he might save us.
This is the LORD for whom we have waited;
let us be glad and rejoice in his salvation.   (Isaiah 25.6–9)

These exquisite lines of an Old Testament prophet furnish us with a
picture of the kingdom of God, the kingdom of God of which Jesus
of Nazareth spoke so often, the kingdom for which he lived and died,
the kingdom that emerges all of a sudden at the end of the Parable of
the Two Brothers.

And so we learn another thing about this parable. Just as God in
the book of Jonah sheds his pantomime costume at the very end and
comes out into the open, so we discover at the very end of The Two
Brothers that God has been hiding himself in the story all along,
dressed in the robes of that fool of a father.

Rejection reinstated

Yet Jesus' followers struggled to come to terms with him. We all still do, of course. No one has yet managed it completely, but some failures are especially tragic. The great Paul takes the stories of Ishmael and Isaac, Esau and Jacob and gives them his own twist. Sacks has this to say about Paul's allegory in Galatians 4.21–31 on the stories of Hagar and Ishmael, Sarah and Isaac:

> Jews are, we say in our prayers several times daily, the children of Abraham, Isaac and Jacob. That is constitutive of Jewish memory, history and identity. Paul argues otherwise. For him, Sarah represents Christianity while Hagar is Judaism. Christians are free, Jews are slaves. Christians are Isaac, Jews are Ishmael. Christians belong, while Jews are to be driven away.
>
> It may be hard for Christians to understand how a Jew feels when he or she reads these texts. It feels like being disinherited, violated, robbed of an identity. This is my past, my ancestry, my story, and here is Paul saying it is not mine at all, it is his and all who travel with him.[37]

In Romans 9 Paul turns to the stories of Esau and Jacob and does something similar, and then something even worse. He argues, as Sacks puts it, that, 'Those who follow Jesus are Jacob. Those who do not, even if they are Jews, are like Esau'.[38] And then he, Paul, quotes that hateful, hate-filled verse of Malachi: 'I have loved Jacob, but I have hated Esau' (see Romans 9.13). He quotes it with approval. He reinstates rejection here, and seats it on the throne of heaven.

And Luke, the only Evangelist to give us the Parable of the Two Brothers, does the same in his own Gospel. It is not certain, alas, that he included in his crucifixion story the words, 'Father, forgive them; for they do not know what they are doing' (Luke 23.34). Many of the earliest and most important manuscripts omit them, and some ancient versions, or translations, also. The NRSV places them inside double square brackets. But no one doubts Luke wrote these verses:

> One of the criminals who were hanged there kept deriding him and saying, 'Are you not the Messiah? Save yourself and us!' But the other rebuked him, saying, 'Do you not fear God, since you are under the same sentence of condemnation? And we indeed have been condemned justly, for we are getting what we deserve for our deeds, but this man has done nothing wrong.' Then he said, 'Jesus, remember me

when you come into your kingdom.' He replied, 'Truly I tell you, today
you will be with me in Paradise.'   (Luke 23.39–43)

One is chosen, the other is rejected, and by Jesus himself, just before
he dies. That is the unmistakable implication. Let us be clear on one
point: the 'derision' of the first criminal, and the words he hurls at
Jesus in his own agony, are *very mild stuff* when we compare them
to the prayers of complaint made in what were Jesus' and Luke's
Scriptures. Moses accuses *God* of much worse than this, and not just
in Exodus 5.[39] As for Job! Yet such prayer in the Old Testament, and
it is there in full measure, is never condemned, not at least by God.
God does not reprimand Moses, but recognizes his hurt, fear and
exhaustion. Job's 16 chapters of railing against God do unnerve his
three companions, and the words of the second criminal in Luke's
passage, 'Do you not fear God?' remind us of them. As Job continues,
the companions lay into him with all the accusations they can muster,
but at the end the author of this great poem has God say to one of
them, 'My wrath is kindled against you and against your two friends;
for you have not spoken of me what is right, as my servant Job has'
(Job 42.7). God knows Job has spoken from the heart, from a heart
that is broken in half. He commends him for his integrity, his per-
sistence, his fearlessness. The book of Job, indeed the Old Testament
as a whole, is on the side of the first criminal, not the second. We
might also say this: the criminal's cry, 'Are you not the Messiah? Save
yourself and us!', is not so different from the accusation the crucified
Jesus himself makes against God in Mark 15.34 and Matthew 27.46,
when he quotes the opening line of Psalm 22, 'My God, my God, why
have you forsaken me?'[40]

Yet these are minor points in the context of what Luke is doing here.
He presents a dying Jesus who chooses one and rejects the other. Like
Paul in Galatians 4 or Romans 9, he is effectively reinstating a God who
chooses one and rejects another. We suspected before, when we came
to those lines we believe he added to the end of the Parable of the Two
Brothers, that he had not grasped the extent of its challenge. His introduction to the parable, his comments on the Pharisees and scribes and
his interpretations of The Lost Sheep and The Lost Coin told a similar
story. Alas, it seems now our suspicions were well founded.

Another case of where we need to look for the gospel beyond the
Gospel.

4

'Here is God: no monarch he, throned in easy state to reign'

———◆◆◆———

Defacing God

Not all the parables in the Gospels are like the Parable of the Two Brothers. There God remains in hiding until the very end, until that line, 'Dear child, you are always with me, and all that is mine is yours.' Sometimes God never emerges. Sometimes God's image is hideously defaced. In Matthew 18 we find what is often called the Parable of the Unforgiving Servant, though that title also leaves something to be desired. It is better to substitute 'Slave' for 'Servant', for a start.

Before it begins Matthew gives us his version of the Parable of the Lost Sheep (no Lost Coin), and then a short section on disciplining members of the Church, which concludes with Peter asking Jesus, 'Lord, if another member of the church sins against me, how often should I forgive? As many as seven times?' To this Jesus replies, 'Not seven times but, I tell you, seventy-seven times' (Matthew 18. 21, 22). Peter's question (like the section on church discipline to which it belongs) clearly stems from the time when Matthew was writing his Gospel, for there was no Church in Jesus' own day. Nevertheless, the terms in which the question is posed, and Jesus' response to it, may well reflect his teaching. Seven times is a lot, and in Jewish thinking would probably have been seen as particularly demanding.[1] *Seventy-seven times* means forgiveness without limit, a forgiveness that knows no bounds. It is an especially significant number, for it occurs in just one other place in the Bible, in Genesis 4.24.

After the poem of creation in Genesis 1 and the tale of the Garden of Eden in chapters 2–3, the narrative almost at once turns to violence, with Cain's murder of his brother Abel. By the time we reach the Flood story, only two chapters later, the earth is said to be 'filled with violence' (Genesis 6.11). In between Cain and the Flood comes a man called Lamech and a terrifying boast to his two wives:

> Adah and Zillah, hear my voice;
>> you wives of Lamech, listen to what I say:
> I have killed a man for wounding me,
>> a young man for striking me.
> If Cain is avenged sevenfold,
>> truly Lamech seventy-sevenfold.
>> (Genesis 4.23–24)

The saying in Matthew 18.22 about forgiving 'seventy-seven times' answers more than Peter's question. It is a reply to Lamech's boast and to the explosion of human violence it symbolizes. It speaks of a new community, a new world, where instead of an escalation of violence, there will be an escalation, a quiet explosion of forgiveness. This world is the one that God sees at the end of Genesis 1 and cries, 'Exceedingly good!'[2] It is the world that Jesus in the Gospels calls 'the kingdom of God' or, more usually in Matthew, 'the kingdom of heaven'. Matthew offers it as an introduction to the parable that follows immediately upon it:

> *For this reason the kingdom of heaven may be compared to* a king who wished to settle accounts with his slaves. When he began the reckoning, one who owed him ten thousand talents was brought to him; and as he could not pay, his lord ordered him to be sold, together with his wife and children and all his possessions, and payment to be made. So the slave fell on his knees before him saying, 'Have patience with me, and I will pay you everything.' And out of pity for him, the lord of that slave released him and forgave him the debt. But that same slave, as he went out, came upon one of his fellow slaves who owed him a hundred denarii; and seizing him by the throat, he said, 'Pay what you owe.' Then his fellow slave fell down and pleaded with him, 'Have patience with me, and I will pay you.' But he refused; then he went and threw him into prison until he should pay the debt. When his fellow slaves saw what had happened, they were greatly distressed, and they went and reported to their lord all that had taken place. Then his lord summoned him and said to him, 'You wicked slave! I forgave you all that debt because you pleaded with me. Should you not have had mercy on your fellow slave, as I had mercy on you?' And in anger his lord handed him over to be tortured until he would pay his entire debt. *So my heavenly Father will also do to every one of you, if you do not forgive your brother or sister from your heart.*   (Matthew 18.23–35)

We have entered a very male world here. This is a 'one-eyed' story, where 'the world is seen through one eye, a male eye'.[3] It is inhabited almost entirely by men, with just one reference to the wife and children of the first slave (the NRSV's 'or sister' of the last verse goes beyond the Greek, which only speaks explicitly of 'your brother'). But that reference only makes things worse, for it counts the man's wife and children among his possessions, dehumanizing them and reducing them to chattels that can be bought and sold, like the rest. Matthew's failure, for whatever reason, to share Luke's pattern, pairing the Parable of the Lost Sheep and its male shepherd with the

Parable of the Lost Coin and its female housewife, is beginning to look significant. In The Two Brothers also the characters are all male, as we noted in the last chapter. But we could replace the father of that story with a mother when it comes to the running up the track to welcome back the younger son, or to the leaving the feast to plead with the elder one, and the story would still work. Indeed they are actions which some of Jesus' hearers might more easily have expected from a mother than a father. We have no hint of feminine overtones in The Unforgiving Slave.

The story is brilliantly told. See how the actions and words of the second slave mirror almost exactly those of the first when they beg for time to pay their debts. Notice the pace of the narrative when the first slave comes upon the second just as soon as he has left the king's presence. We can be fairly confident that buried somewhere in this tale is a parable performed by Jesus. One can well imagine him telling a story to show how God's forgiving us must be mirrored in our own forgiveness of others; if it is not, then we have not taken God's forgiveness into our souls, nor allowed its reality to shape us and determine how we live. Nevertheless, if that is what we might suppose, Matthew's version allows us only to glimpse it through a glass darkly.

The king is a tyrant of huge wealth and unnerving power. The slave who is brought before him owes him a vast sum. It is far too large to be a personal debt. Even allowing for deliberate hyperbole, we have to imagine an official or retainer who is an extremely powerful figure in the king's court, with responsibility for collecting the taxes in a large part of his kingdom. The taxes have proved excessive, however, and the tax collectors under him have failed to deliver, and so he must face the king. We see at once what kind of ruler we are dealing with, when he threatens to sell him and his wife and children. This is a king of absolute power, who can do whatever he likes. At first sight we might think we see another side of him when he has 'pity' on the slave, releases him and forgives the debt, all 10,000 talents of it (millions of pounds in today's currency). After all, we find the same Greek verb in The Two Brothers, when the father sees his younger son returning home and is 'filled with compassion'. And Matthew himself uses it elsewhere: of Jesus' feelings for the crowds of 'harassed and helpless' people (9.36); of his reactions when he sees the crowds of 5,000, then 4,000, who have nothing to eat (14.14, 15.32); of his response when two blind men beg him to have mercy on them (20.34). In each of those four cases the NRSV translates it as 'compassion', so should we not speak of the king's 'compassion' for his official? Perhaps we should, but we must not get carried away. Warren Carter says this:

> Jesus' mercy is constantly expressed in actions which transform and benefit a desperate person. But the king's 'pity' is not of this kind. His decision is calculated for his own benefit. It does not improve the slave's life. In fact, the slave is now even more indebted to him and more easily controlled. His valuable skills and network are not lost to the king so he can accomplish the king's will. And the king has shown magnanimity to at least some of his subjects in not pursuing the amount. But he'll be able to raise other amounts by other means. The king's act is calculated and self-serving, the momentary (v. 34) act of a tyrant.[4]

That might seem a needlessly cynical comment, but when we come to verse 34 at the end of the parable, we may well think it justified. And it would help to explain why the slave acts as he does when he leaves the king's presence. He has lost any freedom he had and feels the king has shamed and humiliated him. He takes it out on the first unfortunate person he comes across. Nothing, however, excuses his actions. He seizes his fellow slave, threatens to strangle him, and when he begs for mercy has no compassion on him at all, but throws him into prison. He is violent, brutal, ruthless. No wonder his fellow slaves are so distressed, and the king so angry when he gets to hear what has happened. How might we interpret that anger? Carter again:

> The king's reaction has to be understood in the . . . context of imperial power. The slave's ruthless act has shamed the king by exposing him to be somewhat soft. While the king's forgiveness of the debt served him well, it could also be interpreted as weakness. In contrast, the slave's act is quite unambiguous. The slave has shown himself to be better at, more ruthless at, the imperial game than the king. Doing so of course dishonours the king . . . The king's response is clear. He revokes his 'pity' and tortures the slave, the perennial punishment of tyrants. Removing the slave . . . shows that the king is not weak but powerful and ruthless.[5]

Let us be clear ourselves. The slave is to be tortured until such time as he pays his entire debt, all those 10,000 talents, millions of pounds. When will that be? 'Never' springs at once to mind. In that case the king is condemning him to be tortured, slowly, relentlessly to death.

This parable, as Matthew presents it, is an ugly tale with no shred of beauty in it. Yet nothing in it is as alarming as the words he uses at its beginning and end, the words we put in italics when we quoted the text. We did that for two reasons: first, to indicate that they do not belong to the story itself, but offer an interpretation of it, almost certainly one of Matthew's own making; second, as is the usual way with italics, to draw attention to them.

'For that reason the kingdom of heaven may be compared to . . . ' How can the parable possibly illustrate the saying about forgiving 'seventy-seven' times? That saying, taken as counterpoise to Lamech's boasting about being avenged 'seventy-sevenfold', envisions a world where forgiveness replaces vengeance and violence, a return to the world of God's making and God's dreaming in Genesis 1. The parable, however, presents a world dominated by vengeance and violence. Though forgiveness features in the story, it is not the forgiveness of which Jesus speaks in his answer to Peter, but one which is manipulative and self-serving.

Yet if Matthew's introduction to the parable is bewildering, his conclusion is disastrous. He ends the parable with the screams of a man being slowly tortured to death, and then adds: 'So my heavenly Father will also do to every one of you, if you do not forgive your brother and sister from your heart.' That turns the parable into a 'text of terror'[6] and its God into a tyrant who has lost all compassion.

There is a similar parable in Matthew 24.45–51, introduced by the words, 'Therefore you also must be ready, for the Son of Man is coming at an unexpected hour' (24.44):

> Who then is the faithful and wise slave, whom his master has put in charge of his household, to give the other slaves their allowance of food at the proper time? Blessed is that slave whom his master will find at work when he arrives. Truly I tell you, he will put that one in charge of all his possessions. But if that wicked slave says to himself, 'My master is delayed,' and he begins to beat his fellow slaves, and eats and drinks with drunkards, the master of that slave will come on a day when he does not expect him and at an hour that he does not know. *He will cut him in pieces and put him with the hypocrites, where there will be weeping and gnashing of teeth.*

That last verse is part of the story. I put it in italics purely for emphasis. Dunn believes both these parables go back to Jesus. Of the last judgement awaiting us he writes,

> That Jesus spoke quite often of such a judgement, and of its outcome in heaven and hell must also be considered very likely. And since the kingdom of God seems to be a way of speaking of heaven, in at least some instances, hell for Jesus was presumably understood as exclusion from the kingdom, with its terrifying consequences.[7]

With reference to Matthew 18.34 he reminds us that 'the torments of hell' were firmly established in the Jewish mind by the time Jesus was born.[8] Snodgrass warns us to allow for hyperbole and not take things too literally:

> A point in a parable may be intended, *not* to mirror theological realities, but to force reflection and analysis. For example, God does not have torturers (Matt. 18.34), nor should we conclude that God is harsh and reaps where he did not sow (Matt. 25.24/Luke 19.21). Both statements serve as hyperbolic warnings.[9]

Drawing together Matthew 18.34 and 24.51, he comments: 'the harshness of some parables of judgement is offensive and troublesome to some' (not then to Snodgrass himself) 'but these parables are not realistic descriptions of judgement. Rather they warn about the reality and seriousness of judgement.'[10]

John Dominic Crossan takes a different line:

> Even within the Gospel versions themselves there is a steady escalation of threats from Jesus, a steady incline in punitive and avenging aspects to his discourse. It seems that the more a Gospel version derives from discrimination or persecution, the more violent is the rhetoric of Jesus within it.[11]

Pointing out that the clause 'where there will be weeping and gnashing of teeth' appears but once in Luke and six times in Matthew, five times at the end of parables, he suggests that Matthew's community was under particular pressure and felt as though they were losing the struggle.[12] He argues that one of the traditions on which Matthew depended, the hypothetical document referred to by scholars as Q, had already changed the God of John the Baptist from non-violent to violent, and had done the same to Jesus and his teaching.[13] In other words, Crossan would argue that the two parables we have quoted from Matthew 18 and 24 do not go back to Jesus, not at least in the form we have them, but stem from the increasingly bitter rhetoric being thrown back and forth by some of the early Christian communities and their opponents, and from the situation of Matthew's community in particular and that of the other communities for which he wrote.

There is no doubt that Matthew knew about active persecution. We only have to look at the end of the Beatitudes at the beginning of the Sermon on the Mount to see that. There are eight blessings pronounced, all of them in poetic form and extremely pithy, in Matthew's Greek even more so than in our English translations. Their speech is disarmingly simple and straightforward, and they establish a rhythm which is sustained almost to the end: 'Blessed are the poor in spirit, for theirs is the kingdom of heaven . . . Blessed are the merciful, for they will receive mercy . . . Blessed are those who are persecuted for righteousness' sake, for theirs is the kingdom of heaven' (Matthew 5.3, 7, 10). But then the rhythm is broken, and the pithiness disappears:

> Blessed are you when people revile you and persecute you and utter all kinds of evil against you falsely on my account. Rejoice and be glad, for your reward is great in heaven, for in the same way they persecuted the prophets who were before you. (5.11)

The Beatitude concerning persecution is given prominence by being placed at the end of the list, as the climax to the series, and is then expanded, as none of the others are, in terms that must surely describe the experiences of Matthew and those for whom he wrote his Gospel. The expansion comes from him, not from Jesus.

So how *are* we to take those words, 'So my heavenly Father will also do to every one of you' and the even more brutal, 'He will cut him in pieces', with its clear reference to the judgement to be exercised by the Son of Man, that is by the risen and triumphant Jesus at the end of time? We do, of course, have to ask questions about possible hyperbole. It is common in the Bible and in the Gospels and the teaching of Jesus – think, for example of that camel trying to squeeze through the eye of a needle in Matthew 19.24. But hyperbole is deliberate exaggeration for effect. Can talk of God ordering someone to be slowly tortured to death, or the implication that the divine Jesus will cut people to pieces, be simply described as exaggeration? Not unless we have already turned God and Jesus into monsters. Snodgrass insists that a verse such as Matthew 18.34 does not mirror theological realities. But in that case what can Matthew possibly mean when he says, 'So my heavenly Father will do to every one of you'? That seems to us a frighteningly unambiguous statement, a claim that the brutal tyranny of the king of the story *does* mirror the reality of God, a suggestion that God can indeed, when push comes to shove, reveal himself as a torturer who has lost all compassion. If that is truly the case, then we Christians had better close the doors of our churches and run for our lives. And we had better keep our mouths firmly shut, for fear of doing harm through our preaching and teaching, since it seems our God is no better than the one whose violence is so enthusiastically preached and acted out by the jihadists of Daesh.

But, of course, that is not true.

The Two Brothers ends effectively with a question, offered on the surface of the story to the elder brother, but really designed for us and for all who hear or read the parable. Are we going to join the party of the kingdom of God? Or are we going to stand on our dignity, remain trapped in our hurt and refuse to go inside? We have those remarkable words, 'Dear child, you are always with me, and all that is mine is yours' to encourage us, but the choice is still ours, and the consequences of its making have to be faced. For if we refuse to join the celebrations for our brother (or sister), then we will remain outsiders, alone, hurt and angry, and our decision will affect all those around us.

Judgement was indeed a part of Jesus' teaching, but in The Two Brothers it is based not on threat and violence, but on bewildering, nonsensical generosity, and on love.

Narrative and counter-narrative: God seated on a throne, or on a mat on the ground?

How could anyone, how could *Matthew*, the Gospel writer who gives us the Sermon on the Mount, come to compare God to a torturer and a tyrant, however terrible the persecution he and his fellow Christians were facing? The imagery is drawn from a dangerous place, from the world of men exercising absolute power, but in the ancient world, including that of Matthew's Judaism and contemporary Roman religion, it was the most common and most influential source of metaphors for those who wished to speak of God. By the late first century, when Matthew wrote his Gospel, that had been the case throughout the ancient Near East for millennia, ever since the invention of monarchy. God, or the gods, had been portrayed as kings, so that kings in their turn could present themselves as living gods or the sons of gods, and then claim absolute authority.

Matthew's Hebrew Scriptures turn again and again to the world of kings when speaking of God. Beyond the metaphors of God as king, judge or warrior, images very closely related to one another, the great Old Testament scholar Walter Brueggemann also discusses those of father, artist, healer, gardener–vinedresser, mother (we will come to that) and shepherd.[14] This does not represent anything like an exhaustive list of the images used of God by the endlessly inventive and imaginative poets and storytellers of the Old Testament, as we will soon discover when we turn to the book of Job. Yet Brueggemann is quick to acknowledge where the emphasis lies, and the dangers that lie therein:

> [I]t is important to recognize that Israel's rhetoric is permeated with 'Yahweh as king' and that Israel's preferred mode of theological discourse is political. Israel's speech about Yahweh is never far removed from issues of power, which are freighted with great temptation and with endless ambiguity.[15]

Perhaps the most famous depiction of God as king in the Hebrew Scriptures is found in Isaiah 6.1–5:

> In the year that King Uzziah died, I saw the Lord sitting on a throne, high and lofty; and the hem of his robe filled the temple. Seraphs were in attendance above him; each had six wings: with two they covered their faces, and with two they covered their feet, and with two they flew. And one called to another and said:

'Holy, holy, holy is the Lord of hosts;
the whole earth is full of his glory.'

The pivots on the thresholds shook at the voices of those who called,
and the house filled with smoke. And I said, 'Woe is me! I am lost, for
I am a man of unclean lips, and I live among a people of unclean lips;
yet my eyes have seen the King, the Lord of hosts!'

In Psalm 89 we find these verses:

For who in the skies can be compared to the Lord?
Who among the heavenly beings is like the Lord,
a God feared in the council of the holy ones,
great and awesome above all that are around him?
O Lord God of hosts,
who is as mighty as you, O Lord?
Your faithfulness surrounds you.
You rule the raging of the sea;
when its waves rise, you still them.
You crushed Rahab like a carcass;
you scattered your enemies with your mighty arm.
(Psalm 89.6–10)

Rahab there has a double reference, to the sea dragon of ancient myth
and to the Egypt of the oppression in Exodus and the brutal tyranny
under which Israel as a people is born and has its childhood. God's
victory in the psalm is the one described in Exodus 14, when he brings
his people out of Egypt and safely through the waters of the Red Sea,
while drowning 'the entire army of Pharaoh' (Exodus 14.28). 'The
Lord tossed the Egyptians into the sea' is the solemn pronouncement
of the narrator in the previous verse. Miriam, Moses' sister, takes her
tambourine in her hand and with all the other women sings a song of
victory, which begins,

Sing to the Lord, for he has triumphed gloriously;
horse and rider he has thrown into the sea.

It includes the lines,

The Lord is a warrior,
the Lord is his name

and it ends with the words,

The Lord will reign for ever and ever.
(Exodus 15.21, 3, 18)[16]

Yet the Bible never speaks with one voice on any matter of significance. We have already mentioned some of the other metaphors used of God in the Old Testament, and there are writers of works within its corpus who turn their backs on images drawn from the court and search for other ways of speaking of God.

The most sustained critique of the language of raw power is found in the book of Job. We had cause to mention Job's railings against God at the end of the last chapter. When his protests begin he is a man who has lost everything, his children, his slaves, his health, his wealth and status in the community, his influence, all his honour and dignity. He sits on the village rubbish heap, scratching his sores. Only his wife and his voice are left to him. His wife, alas, he dismisses as a stupid woman, and we never hear of her again (Job 2.10). But his voice! We hear that loud and very clear. He yells his pain and sense of injustice at God, and then, when he receives no response, he gives up on prayer and shouts into the void. He presumes his suffering comes from God. His three companions, who have come to keep him company and whose presence will quickly add to his distress, believe the same. And all of them start out with the belief in a just God who rewards the righteous and punishes the wicked. The companions stick rigidly to it and, hiding behind their theology books, they abandon compassion and lose sight of Job altogether. One of them, Eliphaz, resorts to inventing a past for Job he never had, in order to turn him into the wicked person that would explain his predicament.

Job himself, to his great credit, is not persuaded. Knowing he has done nothing to deserve his sufferings, he quickly concludes that the wickedness must lie with God. *He* must be the monster. He goes into the attack, using the only weapon he has, his words. The metaphors come thick and fast. He compares God to a wild animal tearing him apart and then hurling his carcass to the jackals; to a thug who smashes him to pieces; to an archer using him as a target; to the commander of an army who batters him with rams as if he were the wall of a city under siege (16.9–14). Raising his eyes to the world at large, he sees all around him the evidence of a God who is a sadistic tyrant, a maniac of terrifying power, who is rampaging round his creation, causing chaos and distress wherever he goes, and who is *enjoying* it (9.2–10: notice the bitter sarcasm of verses 3 and 10; and 9.22–24). Even the animals, birds, plants and fish, he says, will testify to God's cruelty (12.7–9).

The poet who composed this great work is taking the God-language of Isaiah 6, Psalm 89 and Exodus 15 and the rest, giving it a vicious twist, and in the mouth of his hero stretching it to its extremes. But his own critique of it is fundamental. He does not merely condemn the abuse of such royal language. He argues in effect that the court of kings is altogether the wrong place to look to if one wishes to talk of God. That becomes clear when eventually, in chapter 38 of the poem, God breaks his silence and appears to Job. In the longest speeches put into the mouth of God anywhere in the Bible outside the giving of the Torah, he tells of his care for his creation, and he speaks not as a mighty ruler, but as a builder, householder, mother, father or farmer. He builds the foundations of the earth; tucks the sea into bed; takes light and darkness home; inspects the storehouses of the snow and hail; digs irrigation channels in the desert; fathers the rain and the dew; gives birth to the ice and hoarfrost; acts as herdsman or herdswoman to the constellations; gives instructions to storms and lightning, as if to slaves; empties the water-skins of heaven to make it rain; hunts prey for the lions and finds meat for the newly fledged ravens; plays midwife to the ibex and wild deer, unties the wild ass, ploughs the wasteland with the wild ox, guides the migrating eagle, shows the vulture a ledge for her eyrie. The world is not pictured as God's kingdom, but as her household and his farm.

To describe it as *her* household is to go beyond the Hebrew. Nowhere in the Bible, either in the Hebrew of the Old Testament or the Greek of the New, are feminine pronouns used of God. Would they were! And yet because in the households and farms of ancient Israel the duties were shared between husband and wife, when the poet turns to those for his bright imagining of God, inevitably he includes a number of metaphors drawn from women's activities, and many others which are not gender-specific. 'Her household and his farm' (or we might say 'her/his household; her/his farm') conveys his meaning accurately enough, if not the details of his grammar.

So far we have been dealing only with the first speech of God in Job 38–39. There is another, almost as long, in chapters 40–41. It tells of God taking Job to the lairs of Behemoth and Leviathan, the mythical beasts which symbolize the forces of evil and injustice inhabiting the world, to show him the causes of the catastrophes that have overtaken him. Job has been accusing God of being a chaos monster. Now God shows him where the true chaos monsters lie. The poet is drawing here upon an ancient and rich vein of myths about God doing battle with such monsters and destroying them. The verses we have already quoted from Psalm 89 and Exodus 15 make use of similar sources. Isaiah provides us with another example. The prophet calls upon God to rouse himself and come to the rescue of his people, as he did at the Red Sea.

> Awake, awake, put on strength,
>   O arm of the LORD!
> Awake, as in days of old,
>   the generations of long ago!
> Was it not you who cut Rahab in pieces,
>   who pierced the dragon?
> Was it not you who dried up the sea,
>   the waters of the great deep;
> who made the depths of the sea a way
>   for the redeemed to cross over?
>   (Isaiah 51.9–10)

There is Rahab again, and there, too, the image of God cutting his enemy to pieces. Psalm 74.14 speaks of the same event in equally uncompromising language:

> You crushed the heads of Leviathan;
>   you gave him as food for the creatures of the wilderness.

The Hebrew verb translated 'crushed' appears in a strong form in that verse, suggesting 'crushed in pieces'. Marvin Tate, in his commentary on the Psalms, captures its violence when he translates, 'You *smashed* the heads of Leviathan.'[17]

At first the God of Job 40–41 seems to be singing from a similar hymn sheet. God asks Job:

> Have you an arm like God,
>   and can you thunder with a voice like his?
> Deck yourself with majesty and dignity;
>   clothe yourself with glory and splendour.
> Pour out the overflowings of your anger,
>   and look on all who are proud, and abase them.
> Look on all who are proud, and bring them low;
>   tread down the wicked where they stand.
> Hide them all in the dust together;
>   bind their faces in the world below.
>   (Job 40.9–13)

But in our exploration of biblical passages we have been led up the garden path before. That is the case here, also. The poet is deceiving us. As the speech proceeds it emerges that God is describing not only what Job cannot possibly achieve, but also what he, the God of creation, cannot do himself. He is the only one who can face these monsters, but even he has to approach with sword drawn (40.19), and there is no divine slaughter, no dancing in triumph. Though there is talk of possible battle, it is one God dare not provoke. In Job's world, in this God's world, as all too clearly in ours, the dark forces still roam free. The scenery is similar to that in the first speech, a village and its surroundings. We see lotus flowers, reeds and swamps, the taming and domesticating of livestock, fishing; an owner reaching an agreement with a slave, children playing with a pet, traders bartering, steaming cauldrons and smoking rushes, millstones, straw, chaff, potsherds, threshing sledges.

These two speeches are the making of Job. He says to God:

> By the hearing of the ear I had heard of you.
>> But now my eye has seen you.
> Therefore I withdraw my case,
>> and put my dust and ashes behind me.
>
> (42.5–6)[18]

The God Job sees does not live in a palace. His God sits on no throne. His God lives in a village and sits, no doubt, on a mat on the ground. Well, well, what does that remind us of?

God as mother

Before we come to that question and return to the Gospels, let us remember that the two speeches in Job are not entirely unique in the Hebrew Scriptures. They may be unequalled in their sustained rejection of images of God as king or warrior, and in the daring of their portrayal of limits to God's powers, but there are other places where, for example, feminine images are used of God. One of the most remarkable is a bitter prayer of complaint uttered by a Moses who has been bearing the burden of leading his people through the wilderness of Sinai for year upon year upon year, and who has reached the end of his tether. (I use my own translation of the Hebrew; the NRSV, like many of the versions, sounds too polite.)

> Why have you brought disaster upon your servant? . . . To put the burden of this entire people upon me! Am *I* the one who conceived this entire people? Am *I* the one who gave them birth, that you should say to me, 'Carry them in your arms, as a nursing mother carries her suckling child,' until they reach the land you promised on oath to their ancestors? Where shall I find meat to give this entire people? For they weep all over me, saying, 'Give us meat that we may eat!' I cannot carry this entire people all by myself. They are too heavy for me! (Numbers 11.11–14)

Moses compares himself to a mother carrying a demanding, screaming toddler on her hip, and with tight-lipped humour cries, in effect, 'They are too heavy for me, God! *You*, God, are their mother. *You* conceived them and gave them birth. They are *your* responsibility. It's about time you did something about it!' We should not leave this astonishing prayer without noting that one does not talk to kings or mighty warriors like this, let alone tyrants or torturers, not at least without being silenced or put to death. The God of Numbers 11 does not even issue a mild rebuke, but instead comes up with a commendably practical solution of Moses sharing his responsibilities with 70 elders.

More tender are these lines in Isaiah 49.14, where God seeks to comfort the people of Jerusalem:

> Can a woman forget her nursing child,
>> or show no compassion for the child of her womb?
> Even these may forget,
>> yet I will not forget you.
> See, I have inscribed you on the palms of my hands.

141

Then there are the famous words of an earlier prophet, Hosea:

> Yet it was I who taught Ephraim to walk,
>> I took them up in my arms;
>> but they did not know that I healed them.
> I led them with cords of human kindness,
>> with bands of love.
> I was to them like those who lift infants to their cheeks.
>> I bent down to them and fed them . . .
> How can I give you up, Ephraim?
>> How can I hand you over, O Israel? . . .
> My heart recoils within me;
>> my compassion grows warm and tender.
>
>> (Hosea 11.3–4, 8a, c)

Is God father here? Most commentators say so, yet surely Hosea conjures up more easily the picture of God as mother, especially if we translate verse 4b as Helen Schungel-Straumann would have us do:

> And I was for them like those
>> who take a nursling to the breast,
> and I bowed down to him
>> in order to give him suck.[19]

See what happens when we allow the feminine into our God-talk![20]

Returning to the Gospels: first, a prologue and stories of Jesus' birth

So what happens to our picturing God when we turn back to the Gospels? Do we find ourselves immersed once more in the dominant narrative about God as king, or do we discover another counter-narrative? Matthew's Parable of the Unforgiving Slave, and the one in chapter 24 of the Faithful or Unfaithful Slave, belong to the dominant narrative in no uncertain terms, and are particularly ugly expressions of it. Yet our discussions in previous chapters have already begun to paint another picture.

We have quoted some of the lines from John's Prologue already, in our second chapter. We will quote some of those again, and add a verse we did not then include. The lines are more poetry than prose, and once more we will render them as such:

> In the beginning was the Word,
> and the Word was with God,
> and the Word was God.
> He was in the beginning with God.
> All things came into being through him,
> and without him not one thing came into being . . .
> And the Word became flesh
> and pitched tent among us,
> and we have seen his glory
> as of a father's only son,
> full of grace and truth.   (1.1–3b, 14)

All those familiar with this passage will spot at once the change made to the NRSV's translation. That has in its verse 14, 'And the Word became flesh and *lived* among us.' But 'lived' will not do, and the King James Version's 'dwelt' is no better, for they drain the colour from John's Greek. John uses here an unusual verb, *skenoun*, derived from the Greek word for a tent, *skene*. 'Pitched tent' it means, and that is how we should translate it. *Skenoun* appears nowhere else in the Gospels, and its four appearances in Revelation are the only other occurrences in the New Testament (Revelation 7.15, 12.12, 13.6, 21.3). Its relative rarity makes us sit up and take notice, but if we wish to understand its significance, we have to turn to its background in the Old Testament.

In Exodus 25.8–9 God says to Moses: 'And have them' (that is the people, or its craftsmen and craftswomen) 'make me a sanctuary, so that I may dwell with them. In accordance with all that I show you concerning the pattern of the tabernacle and all its furniture, so you shall make it.' 'Tabernacle' could be translated 'tent'. As we read on we find this particular tent is to be very elaborate indeed, with gold upon gold and curtains of the finest materials. Organized religion takes over the narrative, the religion of a settled people whose elite can call upon much wealth. But the narrative context in Exodus suggests something much simpler, something startling and much more profound. For the people in Exodus 25 are in the wilderness beneath Mount Sinai, with God having to keep them alive by 'raining bread from heaven' (Exodus 16.4) and by supplying water struck from rock (17.6). They have fled from Egypt, where they have been slaves under a Pharaoh who has tried to break their backs with hard, unremitting labour. In the Sinai desert they are living in tents (16.16), a migrant, landless people. They have ancient talk of a promised land ringing in their ears, but they despair of ever reaching it. They have come to the sacred mountain, to Mt Sinai, but its summit is hidden in dense cloud and behind the fire of God's glory. Exodus 24 talks of Moses climbing up there, together with his brother Aaron, two of Aaron's sons and 70 of the elders of Israel. There they see God, and there they feast with him (24.9–11). But the more usual story is that Moses climbs the mountain on his own. The narrative reverts to that way of talking immediately, in verse 12. Only he can come into God's presence. That is what these chapters generally maintain. In stunning, unforgettable language, they tell us that God speaks to him 'face to face, as one speaks to a friend' (Exodus 33.11), or that Moses 'soothed God's face' (Exodus 32.11 in a literal translation of the Hebrew), but no one else enjoys such intimacy and the people in general are denied the opportunity. In such a context God's wishing to 'pitch his tent' in the midst of his people is a metaphor of the utmost significance: it brings the glory of God down from the mountain, down to earth; it makes God accessible to all; it denies that God makes himself known only to a spiritual elite. Here God lives not above but among his people, in the midst of their despair, and is able to move on with them when they continue their migration. For a moment we glimpse a remarkable counter-narrative, reminding us of the one supplied by the author of Job.

The essential simplicity of the image is quickly buried in Exodus, but it is reinvigorated by a passage much later in the great narrative, in 2 Samuel. The people of Israel now have a king secure in his own capital of Jerusalem, David no less, with the ark of the covenant, the symbol of God's presence, set in place in a tent specially pitched for it. David, living comfortably in a house of cedar, is embarrassed by his God being only in a tent. He plans to build a temple worthy of his divinity. But 'that same night' the prophet Nathan receives word from God:

> Go and tell my servant David: Thus says the Lord: Are you the one to build me a house to live in? I have not lived in a house since the day I brought up the people of Israel from Egypt to this day, but I have been moving about in a tent and a tabernacle. Wherever I have moved about among all the people of Israel, did I ever speak a word with any of the tribal leaders of Israel, whom I commanded to shepherd my people Israel, saying, 'Why have you not built me a house of cedar?' (2 Samuel 7.5–7)

The temple belongs to the dominant narrative, of God as king, but the tent or tabernacle, in its essential simplicity, speaks of another tale, and it is this tale that John is beginning to tell in his Prologue. Jesus, John claims, has brought the glory of God down to earth. Jesus has brought God near to all, not just to a privileged few. Jesus has made God visible. As God's Word, Jesus has made God audible. And this God lives in a village, and sits on a mat on the ground.

This time we know the name of the village, Nazareth. It is, or was then, a place of a few hundred people – the archaeologists suggest between 200 and 400 – occupying no more than four hectares.[21] It was close to Sepphoris, an important city in the region, and near a road connecting Caesarea on the Mediterranean coast to Tiberias on the Sea of Galilee. But it was not famous. There is no mention of it in the Jewish Scriptures. It was not isolated, but a centre of political, economic and religious power it was not. It was a world away from Isaiah 6; the daily activities of its people would have reminded us of Job 38. And this is the place with which Jesus is forever associated. Nazareth locates him, literally, in the counter-narrative.

If, however, we were to ask people where Jesus came from, whether Christian or not they would probably say Bethlehem. Paul and Mark, the New Testament's two earliest writers, seem not to know of such a tradition. John mentions Bethlehem once. He is describing an argument in a crowd of people listening to Jesus about whether he can possibly be the Messiah when he comes from Galilee. 'Has not the scripture said,' some of them ask, 'that the Messiah is descended from David and comes from Bethlehem, the village where David lived?' (John 7.42). John leaves their question hanging in the air, but most probably he is suggesting, 'Aha! They think Jesus comes from Galilee and so cannot be the Messiah. But in fact, he *does* come from Bethlehem! And he *is* the Messiah!'[22] But, of course, it is Matthew and Luke who are responsible for our linking Jesus with Bethlehem. And their stories of Jesus' birth surely belong firmly to the counter-narrative. Do they not talk of Jesus being born in a filthy stable and laid in a manger, after his mother Mary and Joseph have been refused lodging? And do not Mary and Joseph have to pick him up and hurry out into the night to avoid him being killed by Herod's soldiers, and then take him all the way to Egypt to find sanctuary? Born in utter poverty, rejected, his parents turned away; his small life threatened, becoming a refugee when he is but days old: he could hardly be further from the comforts, security and privileges of the courts of kings.

And that is precisely one of the reasons why the birth stories make such an impact. They declare that Jesus is one of us. He is not high and mighty, nor out of touch with 'the real world'. Quite the reverse, he is among the most vulnerable, and so he understands our own vulnerabilities. And that means that God understands them, also.

But what we have summarized as the Christmas story bears closer relation to nativity plays, carols and hymns than to the narratives we find in Matthew or Luke. Those narratives are very different from one another, in their detail, their tone, even their casting. In Matthew Mary and Joseph do not have to travel to Bethlehem, for Bethlehem is where they live. Jesus in Matthew is born safely at home. The reason why they have to leave Bethlehem is because some magi have travelled from the east seeking a child who has been born, they say, as the new king of the Jews. Alas, most unwisely they say it openly to everyone they meet in Jerusalem, where there is already a king of the Jews, and a ruthless and paranoid one at that. Herod immediately concludes that this new king is the Messiah, the one who would seek to restore the old monarchy descended from King David, and do so, as most people then believed, through brute force. Herod, who is not descended from David, decides to nip the problem in the bud.

He has an audience with the magi and learns from his own experts that the Messiah is expected to be born at Bethlehem, a village not in distant Galilee but alarmingly close to Jerusalem, just five miles or so to the south. He sends in his troops, with orders to kill all children in the village two years old and under. He is taking no chances. Joseph and Mary (with Matthew we should really put them that way round, for Joseph throughout plays the major role) get out just in time, taking the newborn Jesus with them. Immediately pictures spring to our minds of the mothers and fathers of our own day fleeing Syria, Iraq or Afghanistan with babies or small children in their arms.

Joseph, Mary and Jesus find themselves refugees in Egypt, this time, unlike the Egypt of the early chapters of Exodus, a safe place for Jews to be. But it is not home. So, when they hear that Herod has died, they decide to go back. However, they cannot return to Bethlehem, for Herod's son Archelaus is in power, and they fear he will be as bad as his father. They end up in Nazareth, and so, by a long, dangerous and roundabout route, Jesus becomes Jesus of Nazareth.

Luke, as we all know, begins the story of Jesus' birth in Nazareth, for that, not Bethlehem, is Mary and Joseph's home village. (In Luke Mary definitely comes first; it is Joseph this time who remains in the shadows.) While Matthew faces the problem of getting Jesus from Bethlehem to Nazareth, Luke has to get him from Nazareth to Bethlehem for his birth. While Jesus in Matthew is born against the background of Herod and the brutal exercise of power in Jerusalem, Luke places his birth in the context of a worldwide census conducted by the Roman Emperor Augustus. Luke puts Jesus on a larger stage.

Matthew's stories of Jesus' birth are dark and full of fear.

> Matthew's fragile Jesus is a candle in a dark world, where the breeze of human frailty [the magi] and the storm of men's concern for their power and honour [Herod and his soldiers] threaten to blow out its flame, and so nearly, so nearly succeed.[23]

Luke's birth stories are full of light, and yet Augustus casts a shadow over the narrative at one point. He clicks his finger in distant Rome for the census to be taken, and a young girl, heavily pregnant, has to travel some 85 miles so that the man to whom she is betrothed can get his name on the imperial list. She is carrying her first child. She has to leave behind her own family and the local women who would normally help her in her labour, and travel to a community she has never seen before. Luke mentions no donkey for her to ride on for the journey. Augustus and his version of imperial power put her at risk, and her unborn child, too. She will not have time to return to Nazareth for the birth.

The nativity plays tell another tale. They present the greatest dangers for Mary and her child after they reach Bethlehem. In truth Luke places those dangers, if we will but use our imaginations, on the journey, and they arise, not from the supposedly inhospitable people of Bethlehem, but from Augustus. For the people of Bethlehem do not turn Mary and Joseph away. Luke, it is true, does not spell out their hospitality, but he does not need to. The hearers of his Gospel would have assumed Joseph's relatives take them in, for Bethlehem is where Joseph's family comes from. They do not have to turn to an inn and then find no room. Almost certainly there were no inns in Bethlehem and Luke's Greek is mistranslated. What he most probably means is that the house of Joseph's relatives is small, and that its family cannot find a private area large enough for the birth and for the baby once he is born, so Mary must go into labour in the part of the house reserved for their domestic animals and must use their manger and its straw to lie her baby down to sleep. Luke mentions no stable, let alone a filthy one. There is no rejection, no knocking on doors and being turned away. Instead we must imagine warm, generous hospitality and a poor family doing its best, with the local midwife called for if there is one, and the women of the neighbouring houses doing what they can to help.[24]

And yet, of course, we *are* here a long way from the comforts and privileges of the courts of kings or emperors. Luke might seem to emphasize that in his description of the first people to visit Jesus after his birth: they are shepherds, 'living in the fields, keeping watch over their flocks by night' (Luke 2.8). That means they are not from the village, or else they would have brought their flocks back to the communal pens for the night. They are not from any village. They are nomads. Today we would call them Bedouin. Imagine nomadic shepherds being the first to greet the birth of an Augustus, or a new Herod for that matter! Or does Luke want us to think of King David? Not only was Bethlehem David's home village, but when we first meet him in the narrative of 1 Samuel he is out in the fields 'keeping the sheep' (1 Samuel 16.11). There is a measure of ambiguity here.

The equivalent story in Matthew is more ambiguous still. The magi travel from the east looking for a king. Some nativity plays have them being led by a star straight to Bethlehem. Not so in Matthew. At first they go to the wrong place. Seeking a king of the Jews, they go to where they might expect to find one. They go to Jerusalem, the centre of political, economic and military power in the region. It is only when Herod's Jewish advisors tell them the Messiah is to be born in Bethlehem that they move on and follow the star the last few miles of their journey. So they do not find Jesus in a palace, or even in the capital city. And yet they have observed a new star at its rising, and Matthew was writing his Gospel after stories had been told about strange celestial phenomena accompanying the births of the Roman emperors Augustus, Tiberius and Nero. And they do bring very expensive gifts with them, gold, frankincense and myrrh. These are gifts fit for a king, and Matthew does not say that Mary and Joseph have no idea what to do with them. In presenting them the magi kneel before the baby and his mother and pay him homage.

So it seems clear Matthew does wish us to see Jesus as a king, after all. Not just any king, either, certainly not a successor to Herod, an addition to his dynasty. Jesus is descended from David. Jesus is the longed-for Messiah. The very first verse of Matthew's Gospel reads: 'An account of the genealogy of Jesus the Messiah, the son of David, the son of Abraham.' And that is why he must have Jesus born in Bethlehem. Nazareth will not do. It has no connections with David. We will recall that when Peter says to Jesus, 'You are the Messiah', it is Matthew who has Jesus heap such praise on him (Matthew 16.16–18). Mark's version of the episode is much more ambiguous, to the extent that it is not clear whether Jesus accepts the title or not, and Luke, who will often treat Mark's text with greater freedom than Matthew, here follows him almost to the letter (Mark 8.29–31; Luke 9.20–22).

Luke is, however, just as keen as Matthew to establish Jesus' royal credentials. At the point in his birth stories where he explains why Mary and Joseph travel to Bethlehem, he writes, 'Joseph also went from the town of Nazareth in Galilee to Judea, *to the city of David called Bethlehem, because he was descended from the house and family of David.* He went to be registered with Mary . . .' (2.4–5a). Later, when Mary and Joseph take Jesus to the Temple in Jerusalem 'to present him to the Lord', they meet with an old man called Simeon, to whom, Luke tells us, 'It had been revealed . . . by the Holy Spirit that he would not see death before he had seen the Lord's Messiah' (2.26). When Simeon sees Jesus, he at once recognizes him for who he is, takes him in his arms and sings his famous song of celebration, a song of his own fulfilment and contentment .

These birth narratives, whether Matthew's or Luke's, seem to pull both ways, declaring Jesus a king while placing him among the poor. Yet we must remember that many who attained great power in the ancient world, as in our own, came from very humble beginnings. Is not David out with the sheep when Samuel the king-maker calls on Jesse in Bethlehem, to anoint one of his sons king? Jesse makes seven of his sons pass before him, but Samuel recognizes that none of them is the man God is looking for. 'Are all your sons here?' he asks. 'There remains yet the youngest, but he is keeping the sheep,' Jesse replies (1 Samuel 16.11). No one thinks that *David* could be the one. But of course he is. And the rest, as they say, is history.

So the circumstances of Jesus' birth, in both Matthew and Luke, may be deceptive. If he is a king, as they both say he is, then one day he might find himself walking the corridors of power.

In the end he does, but they are the corridors of the high priest in Jerusalem, who with the rest of the Temple's hierarchy condemn him as deserving death; the palace of another Herod, where he is taken for the contempt and mockery of him and his soldiers (a story told only by Luke, in 23.6–12); and finally the headquarters of Pilate the Roman governor, who condemns him to be crucified, the most degrading and humiliating form of execution in his repertoire.

And so the story of Jesus of Nazareth comes to a close. Except that it does not, of course. We must remind ourselves of some of the features of the Evangelists' stories about Jesus between his birth and his death, and of Jesus' own teaching we find there, and then return with the women disciples to the resurrection. Do these support the dominant narrative of Jesus and God himself as king? Just because Jesus is crucified does not mean otherwise. Just as there were kings and rulers in the ancient world who rose to great power from obscurity, so there were plenty who came to a sticky end. Yet might we find again a gospel beyond the Gospels?

'I am among you as one who serves'

At the centre of Jesus' own teaching is 'the kingdom of God', and that, as we have remarked before, suggests the image of God as king. Nevertheless, it is a kingdom far removed from those of either Herod or Augustus. It is one where, to quote Matthew's version of the saying, 'the last will be first, and the first will be last' (Matthew 20.16). And its citizens are to love their enemies. In the book of Proverbs we find the remarkable saying:

> If your enemies are hungry, give them bread to eat;
> and if they are thirsty, give them water to drink;
> for you will heap coals of fire on their heads,
> and the LORD will reward you.
> (Proverbs 25.21–22)

Jesus famously picks up these words and runs with them:

> You have heard that it was said, 'You shall love your neighbour and hate your enemy.' But I say to you, Love your enemies and pray for those who persecute you, so that you may be children of your Father in heaven; for he makes his sun rise on the evil and on the good, and sends rain on the righteous and on the unrighteous. For if you love those who love you, what reward do you have?   (Matthew 5.43–46a)

In this kingdom not only is God king, but Jesus, as son of David, Messiah, Christos,[25] Christ, mirrors the kingship of God, or so all the Gospels claim. Though in Mark Jesus seems reluctant to accept the title Messiah from Peter in 8.30, after his arrest, when the high priest asks him, 'Are you the Messiah, the Son of the Blessed One?' he replies, 'I am' (Mark 14.61–62a). And if Matthew and Luke seek to establish his royal credentials at the very beginning of their Gospels, so does John in his. Jesus' status as Messiah is clearly implied by John the Baptist, who says he is 'not worthy to untie the thong of his sandal' (John 1.20–27), and is declared openly by Andrew, who tells his brother Peter, 'We have found the Messiah' (1.41).

And, of course, after his death Jesus became known by all his followers as 'the Christ', or simply 'Christ', and we are 'Christians' to this day.

But if Jesus is king, he does not behave like one. Storyteller and poet, yes; rabbi, healer, prophet (we will soon come to that), all these, but king, never. Instead he embraces the status and practice of a slave.

151

We have already seen how he responds to the male disciples, whenever they are caught arguing about which of them is or will be the greatest. We need to quote once more those words in Luke 22.25–27:

[H]e said to them, 'The kings of the Gentiles lord it over them; and those in authority over them are called benefactors. But not so with you; rather the greatest among you must become like the youngest, and the leader like one who serves. For who is greater, the one who is at the table or the one who serves? Is it not the one at the table? *But I am among you as one who serves.'*

Ten chapters earlier Luke includes what is very nearly a parable. Jesus says to his disciples:

Be dressed for action and have your lamps lit; be like those who are waiting for their master to return from the wedding banquet, so that they may open the door for him as soon as he comes and knocks. Blessed are those slaves whom the master finds alert when he comes; truly I tell you, *he will fasten his belt and have them sit down and eat, and he will come and serve them.*   (12.35–37)

There is a famous passage in the *Epistulae Morales* of Seneca, a Roman Stoic philosopher and writer who was for a time a contemporary of Jesus, though Jesus was dead long before the *Epistulae* were written.

I'm glad to learn, from visitors of yours who come here, that you live on friendly terms with your slaves. That squares with your sensible outlook no less than with your philosophy. 'They're slaves.' Perhaps, but still fellow human beings. 'They're slaves.' But they share your roof. 'They're slaves.' Friends, rather – humble friends. 'They're slaves.' Well fellow slaves, if you reflect that Fortune has an equal power over them and you. That's why I laugh at those who think it derogatory to dine with their slaves.   (From *Epistulae Morales* 47)

There is much in this passage to admire, even if Jesus would never have spoken of people as slaves to Fortune; they were instead children of their Father God. But, of course, for a master to dine with his slaves is not the same as changing roles with them, so that they become the honoured members of the household and he becomes their slave. Seneca, at his most enlightened, would surely have found Jesus' near-parable bewildering, indeed shocking. 'So the last will be first, and the first will be last.' That is not what Seneca, who was decidedly one of the 'first' in his society, meant at all.

And then, of course, there is that moment in John 13 when, taught by Mary of Bethany, Jesus

> got up from the table, took off his outer robe, and tied a towel around himself. Then he poured water into a basin and began to wash the disciples' feet and to wipe them with the towel that was tied around him. (John 13.4–5)

Luke's near-parable is turned into action.

The Gospels are thickly peopled with men, women and children who find a new dignity, honour and status, often ones of which they have never dreamed, through their encounters with Jesus, precisely because he acts as their slave. 'I am among you as one who serves.' They leave his presence knowing exactly what those words mean.

Riding into Jerusalem

Yet what about that procession into Jerusalem, the one Christians celebrate every Palm Sunday? Surely here we see Jesus riding into the holy city of Jerusalem as a king? The story is in all four Gospels. We will quote the text of the earliest of them, Mark:

> When they were approaching Jerusalem, at Bethphage and Bethany, near the Mount of Olives, he sent two of his disciples and said to them, 'Go into the village ahead of you, and immediately as you enter it, you will find there a colt that has never been ridden; untie it and bring it. If anyone says to you, "Why are you doing this?" just say this, "The Lord needs it and will send it back here immediately." ' They went away and found a colt tied near a door, outside in the street . . . Then they brought the colt to Jesus and threw their cloaks on it; and he sat on it. Many people spread their cloaks on the road, and others spread leafy branches that they had cut in the fields. Then those who went ahead and those who followed were shouting,
>
> > 'Hosanna!
> > Blessed is the one who comes in the name of the Lord!
> > Blessed is the coming kingdom of our ancestor David!
> > Hosanna in the highest heaven!'
>
> Then he entered Jerusalem and went into the temple; and when he had looked around at everything, as it was already late, he went out to Bethany with the twelve. (Mark 11.1–11)

The details of this procession, as Mark describes it, clearly present it as a royal event, including the use of the colt (see Zechariah 9.9 and Genesis 49.11) and the cloaks spread on the road (see 2 Kings 9.13). The lines sung by his followers begin with words from Psalm 118.26: 'Blessed is the one who comes in the name of the Lord' (and the next verse includes the line, 'Bind the festal procession with branches'). That particular psalm was not originally written for the triumphal entry of a king to Jerusalem, but for the welcoming of pilgrims to the Temple. But when Mark's crowd then adds, 'Blessed is the coming kingdom of our ancestor David!' they undoubtedly turn the welcoming of pilgrims into the welcoming of a king. In Matthew's version the crowd leave us in no doubt at all:

> Hosanna to the Son of David!
> Blessed is the one who comes in the name of the Lord!

Hosanna in the highest heaven.
(Matthew 21.9)

And a few verses before that, as preparations are being made for the procession, Matthew interrupts the narrative by quoting Zechariah:

> Tell the daughter of Zion,
> Look, your king is coming to you,
>   humble, and mounted on a donkey,
>   and on a colt, the foal of a donkey.
>   (Matthew 21.5)[26]

Matthew has omitted the second line of Zechariah's verse, which reads,

> Lo, your king comes to you;
>   *triumphant and victorious is he.*

Encouraged by that omission, some commentators draw our attention to the next verse in the Zechariah passage, emphasizing how the prophet speaks of a king coming for peace, not war:[27]

> He will cut off the chariot from Ephraim
>   and the warhorse from Jerusalem;
> and the battle-bow shall be cut off,
>   and he shall command peace to the nations.
>   (Zechariah 9.10)

But their argument begins to look rather thin if we read just a little further. Zechariah concludes 9.13 with the lines,

> I will arouse your sons, O Zion,
>   against your sons, O Greece,
>   and wield you like a warrior's sword.

He expands the metaphor of God as warrior and gets into his stride with this:

> the Lord God will sound the trumpet
>   and march forth in the whirlwinds of the south.
> The LORD of hosts will protect them,
>   and they shall devour and tread down the slingers;
> they shall drink their blood like wine,
>   and be full like a bowl,
>   drenched like the corners of the altar.   (9.14b–15)

Peace in this passage has quickly turned into disgusting violence, enabled by God himself.

What then does Jesus do when he enters Jerusalem? In Mark's version of the story, he looks around . . . and then goes back to Bethany! Complete anti-climax. In that case what on earth was the procession about? What was the point of it?

Are we to recall that the festival of the Passover is approaching, that the city will be filling up with pilgrims, and that Jesus' grand procession into the city will not have been the only one? The Roman governor, Pontius Pilate, will be riding in on his warhorse, accompanied by cavalry and foot soldiers, come to reinforce the garrison of the Antonia Fortress, overlooking the Temple precincts, come to keep the peace at time of festival. The Passover is the worst time of year for a Roman governor of Judea. Not only is Jerusalem packed with people, but they are there to remember God's bringing them out of Egypt through the Red Sea and the destruction of the Egyptian army and its Pharaoh in its waters. For Egypt, read Rome. The connection will not be hard for people to make. Pilate knows that. It will only take one to start a riot. Pilate knows that, too. So he makes sure his procession is suitably intimidating.

Marcus Borg and John Dominic Crossan picture its sights and sounds:

> A visual panoply of imperial power: cavalry on horses, foot soldiers, leather armour, helmets, weapons, banners, golden eagles mounted on poles, sun glinting on metal and gold. Sounds: the marching of feet, the creaking of leather, the clinking of bridles, the beating of drums. The swirling of dust. The eyes of the silent onlookers, some curious, some awed, some resentful.[28]

With an added touch of drama, they speak of Pilate and Jesus riding into the city on the same day, Jesus from the east, Pilate, having come up from Caesarea on the coast, from the west.[29] We do not have to insist on that degree of coincidence to argue that Jesus is deliberately aping Pilate, but riding a young colt rather than a warhorse (in line with Zechariah Matthew has him on a donkey, and John on a little donkey), and with no armour, no weapons, no banners or insignia in sight. Call it what we will, acted parable, street theatre, political protest, daring parody, and it is all those things, it is neither a demonstration of power nor a bid for control. It is not meant to intimidate anyone, nor start a riot. But it is meant to make Pilate sit up in his saddle and take notice. It is meant to challenge his understanding of power, and the way he exercises it through fear and the threat of force. It seems, alas, that the point struck home only too well.

Mayhem in the Temple

If we have understood Jesus' procession aright, then it is more the action of a prophet than a king, however much the Evangelists have written it up as a royal event. Matthew concludes his version of it with the words, 'The crowds were saying, "This is the prophet Jesus from Nazareth in Galilee" ' (21.11). The crowds are spot on! Actions can speak louder than words, and the Old Testament prophets sometimes acted out their prophecies for greater effect. In causing a major disturbance in the Jerusalem Temple, Jesus should again be understood as playing a prophetic role, one familiar to his Jewish contemporaries. He does not just proclaim the coming destruction of the Temple and the end of its worship, but he acts it out. This certainly seems how Luke understands his action. He follows his description of the procession towards the city with this:

> As he came near and saw the city, he wept over it, saying, 'If you, even you, had only recognized on this day the things that make for peace! But now they are hidden from your eyes. Indeed, the days will come upon you, when your enemies will set up ramparts around you and surround you, and hem you in on every side. They will crush you to the ground, you and your children within you, and they will not leave within you one stone upon another; because you did not recognize the time of your visitation from God.' Then he entered the temple and began to drive out those who were selling things there.   (Luke 19.41–45)

Luke has composed Jesus' lament in the light of the Roman army's siege of Jerusalem and their destruction of the city in AD 70, and (with a lack of plausibility, but with alarming theology) he finds the reason for that disaster in the refusal of so many Jews to embrace Christ. Yet he still manages to throw light on what Jesus does in the Temple: he speaks of destruction, and then he turns his words into dramatic action.

Luke's version of the disturbance in the Temple is very brief. Mark's is more detailed. After spending the night in Bethany Jesus returns to the city, goes to the Temple and there, Mark says,

> he began to drive out those who were selling and those who were buying in the temple, and he overturned the tables of the money-changers and the seats of those who sold doves; and he would not allow anyone to carry anything through the temple.   (Mark 11.15–16)

Those final words are the most significant, for they mean Jesus is disrupting everything and preventing the work of the Temple from continuing. John, who alone puts the story near the start of Jesus' ministry, adds that Jesus drove out the animals that had been brought for sacrifice (John 2.15).

Early in the sixth century AD, at a time of great political and military crisis for Jerusalem and Judah, when they were threatened by the Babylonians, the prophet Jeremiah demonstrated what he believed the outcome would be. He tells of what God has instructed him:

> Thus said the LORD: Go and buy a potter's earthenware jug. Take with you some of the elders of the people and some of the senior priests, and go out to the valley of the son of Hinnom at the entry of the Potsherd Gate, and proclaim there the words that I tell you. You shall say . . .Thus says the LORD of hosts, the God of Israel: I am going to bring such disaster upon this place that the ears of everyone who hears of it will tingle . . . Then you shall break the jug in the sight of those who go with you, and shall say to them: Thus says the LORD of hosts: So will I break this people and this city, as one breaks a potter's vessel, so that it can never be mended.   (Jeremiah 19.1–3a, 3c, 10–11)[30]

The mayhem Jesus causes in the Temple belongs firmly in this tradition. It is the act of a Jewish prophet, not a king. A king would never have acted on his own, and there would have been much more than the removal of animals, the disruption of liturgy and sacrifice, and the overturning of tables. Much blood would have been spilled and many lives lost.

His actions are enough, however, together with the procession before it, to alarm the Temple authorities, and to persuade Pilate he must get rid of Jesus. He must do so quickly. He must make a public example of him, as a warning to others. He need not arrest his followers, because he is clearly not intent on violence, but he himself, as the leader of the movement, must go. He must crucify him. Another piece, he thinks, of Jewish trash.

No sticky end

'Just as there were kings and rulers in the ancient world who rose to great power from obscurity, so there were plenty who came to a sticky end.' That is what we said. Pilate declares Jesus 'King of the Jews' (Mark 15.2, 9, 12, 26), and his soldiers follow suit (15.18; there are parallels in the other three Gospels), but they do so with irony and bitter mockery, deriding both Jesus himself and his followers. They suppose, that whatever his true ambition might have been, they have brought him to a very sticky end indeed.

The Gospels do not agree with them. All four spend much time on Jesus' death. Their narratives move inexorably towards it, and the tension increases page by page until they reach Golgotha. The crucifixion itself they describe with great restraint, though Matthew gets carried away for a moment, with his talk of earthquake and tombs opening and their dead emerging. But they all present it as a moment of fulfilment, of blinding revelation (if revelation can be blinding in the pitch dark) and of the triumph of God. John calls it Jesus' 'hour'. The Pharisee Paul, writing before any of the Evangelists, famously says, 'Jews demand signs and Greeks desire wisdom, but we proclaim Christ crucified' (1 Corinthians 1.22–23a). It is this proclamation that makes Christianity distinctive.

The whole of 1 Corinthians 1.23 reads, 'but we proclaim Christ crucified, a stumbling-block to Jews and foolishness to Gentiles'. The Greek word Paul uses for 'stumbling-block' is *scandalon*. It is not just those Jews who did not join the Church, or their Gentile contemporaries, who could not come to terms with the crucifixion of Jesus. Christians failed also. We still fail. In Paul's letter to the Philippians he quotes a hymn which already belonged to the Church's worship. If, as scholars think, Philippians was written in the mid to late 50s or early 60s, then this hymn is indeed one of the earliest Christian compositions to have survived:

Let the same mind be in you that was in Christ Jesus,

who, though he was in the form of God,
did not regard equality with God
as something to be exploited,
but emptied himself,
taking the form of a slave,
being born in human likeness.

And being found in human form,
    he humbled himself
    and became obedient to the point of death –
    even death on a cross.
Therefore God also highly exalted him
    and gave him the name
    that is above every name,
so that at the name of Jesus
    every knee should bend,
    in heaven and on earth and under the earth,
and every tongue should confess
    that Jesus Christ is Lord,
    to the glory of God the Father.
                                    (Philippians 2.5–11)

This is a magnificent and very beautiful poem, of course it is. However, it makes a fundamental error. It claims that God is not *really* like Jesus. Jesus appeared as a slave but God is a king, always has been, always will be. To reveal God on earth, it seems to say, Jesus had to empty himself of God. But after his death, when God exalted him and gave him back all the trappings of a heavenly king, all was well again and the divine equilibrium restored. And all must now bend the knee.

Yet suppose we stand at Golgotha, look into the face of the crucified Jesus and say, 'That *is* what God is like.' And what if God himself does *not* play king, never has, never will? What if God washes feet? What if it is *God* who bends the knee?

Resurrection

How can the Gospels possibly represent Jesus' degrading, humiliating death as his finest hour, indeed as God's finest hour? In the first instance, it is because of the stories told by Mary of Magdala and others among the women disciples, or rather because of the experiences they related, experiences which came to be shared by the men, and by Paul himself. To put it simply, they met Jesus again, and in doing so knew they had reached into the heart of the divine. None of them were witnesses to the resurrection itself. Over that, in all their Easter stories, the Gospels draw a veil. The Evangelists knew full well that the resurrection was beyond all describing and beyond all imagining. Yet Jesus was once more present to the disciples, in a way he had not been before. That the Evangelists make plain. Now his friends saw him for who he was. It was another Transfiguration, this time for all of them. He was not a ghost, or simply a man come to life again, but a man who had slipped out of death and now wore the very life of God.

Mary of Magdala, in John's compelling story of her encounter with the risen Jesus, struggles to recognize him, and no wonder! At first, when she sees him, she thinks he is the gardener, then when he calls her name she addresses him as 'My rabbi!' But when she runs back to the other disciples, she cries, 'I have seen the Lord!' (John 20.18). She means 'I have seen God!' A few verses later, when Jesus appears among the disciples, including the men, Thomas cries out, 'My Lord and my God!' (20.28). His words bring John's Gospel to a close, at least to a conclusion in 20.30–31. (The narrative reopens, and continues for another chapter.)

In that story of Thomas John emphasizes that the risen Jesus still bears the marks of crucifixion, and Luke does the same when he speaks of Jesus appearing to his disciples (Luke 24.36–43). The Lukan passage is the most superficial of the Gospels' resurrection stories, and Luke's purpose is simply to counter any notion that the disciples were seeing a ghost.[31] But John's story is of a different order. If we take it up and place it over the text of his story of the crucifixion, we see why John regards Jesus' dying as the moment when the life of God is revealed. 'When you lift up the Son of Man,' Jesus says of himself back in John 8.28, 'then you will know that I am.' We have kept closer to John's Greek there than the NRSV does, for a simpler translation allows us to catch the mysterious 'I am', the echo of the divine name that God gives Moses at the Burning Bush in Exodus 3.14. For John the 'lifting up' of the Son of Man is a reference to the resurrection and to what he calls his 'ascending to the Father' (see 20.17). Yet in the first instance it means the crucifixion. 'And I, when I am lifted up from the earth, will draw all people to myself,' John has Jesus say in 12.32. And then he adds, 'He said this to indicate the kind of death he was to die' (12.33). For John the crucifixion, the resurrection and ascension are all of a piece. The resurrection and ascension are commentary on the crucifixion. It is the death which is the supreme Moment of Truth. The crucifixion is not left behind in the resurrection, let alone annulled. The marks of the nails make that plain. Rather, the thick darkness of Jesus' death is seen shining with the glory of God. It is a paradox to beat all paradoxes.

Metaphor matters

What if God washes feet? What if it is God who bends the knee? Let us make ourselves clear. We are not saying that God *literally* washes feet or literally bends his knee. After all, God has no knee to bend. God is Other; God is Beyond; God is the Mystery that both embraces and informs the universe of which we human beings are so very small a part. There is, in fact, nothing we can say about God that is literally true. With God we always have to resort to metaphor, to poetic speech or storytelling, to music or the visual arts.

Yet the metaphors we choose, the narratives we tell and tell again, the pictures we create, the music we play when we seek to capture the sounds of heaven, these matter, and matter hugely. We need, alas, no reminding of that in this, the early part of the twenty-first century. One only has to consider the jihadists of Daesh, the passages of the Qur'an to which they turn, the things they do in the name of God. We only have to recall how fervently many Christian fundamentalists in the United States supported George Bush when he stormed into Iraq in the name of their God, or listen to the fear- and hate-filled rhetoric they are using to this day in support of the extreme right of or beyond the Republican Party. No wonder so many people are scared stiff of religion and believe it is irredeemably toxic.

Reflecting on the disasters Jews suffered at the hands of the Romans in the first and second centuries AD, Jonathan Sacks says this: 'What Jews discovered when they had lost almost everything else was that *religion can survive without power*.'[32] Western Christianity, he continues, has had to learn the same lesson, although we might add that some Christians are trying very hard to unlearn it. '*You cannot impose truth by force*', he writes, and 'That is why religion and power are two separate enterprises that must never be confused.'[33]

That is why we Christians must examine very carefully the ways in which we portray our God. When our forebears were living in those early decades after Jesus' death, and still considered themselves Jews or, as Gentile converts, members of the family of Judaism, they had as their inheritance in the Hebrew Scriptures both the dominant narrative of God as king and warrior, and a powerful counternarrative which did not draw its inspiration from the courts of kings, but had God as mother, or sitting on a mat on the ground. Despite Jesus of Nazareth, what he taught and what he did, the way he lived and the way he died, they never entirely abandoned the dominant narrative – remember Matthew's Parable of the Unforgiving Slave or that hymn in Philippians – and when after Constantine their successors found themselves walking the corridors of power, then they picked it up and cherished it, enshrined it in their worship and liturgies and, to the great hurt of millions over the centuries, let it loose in their practice.

It is time to return to the Gospels – it always has been, but there is a particular urgency in our day – to hear again their extraordinary counter-narrative, knowing full well how radical and challenging it is.

The title of this chapter is taken from a hymn composed by Bill Vanstone, one of my predecessors at Chester Cathedral when I was working there, though better known for his inspiring work as a parish priest. The hymn is 'Morning glory, starlit sky', and its words form a conclusion to his much loved book, *Love's Endeavour, Love's Expense*, published in 1977. It is perhaps one of the greatest hymns in the English language. Its last two verses are these:

> Therefore he who shows us God
> helpless hangs upon the tree;
> and the nails and crown of thorns
> tell of what God's love must be.
>
> Here is God: no monarch he,
> throned in easy state to reign;
> here is God, whose arms of love
> aching, spent, the world sustain.

We might say this last chapter of our book has ended up as a commentary on those lines. We must let their words sink deep into our minds and our souls, and allow them to influence and to challenge how we live and how as Christian communities we behave.

Notes

———•◦•———

1 'Do you see this woman?'

1 Kurt Aland, Matthew Black, Carlo M. Martini, Bruce M. Metzger and Allen Wikgren (eds), *The Greek New Testament*, 3rd edn (United Bible Societies, Swindon, 1983), p. 234; Wayne A. Meeks (gen. ed.), *The HarperCollins Study Bible, New Revised Standard Version* (HarperCollins, New York, 1989), p. 1971.

2 Amy-Jill Levine and Marc Zvi Brettler (eds), *The Jewish Annotated New Testament, New Revised Standard Version* (OUP, New York, 2011), p. 116.

3 We need to be cautious about Luke's portrayal of Simon. The Pharisees are undoubtedly demonized in the Gospels, including Luke's. We will discuss that further in our next chapter.

4 Barbara E. Reid, 'Do You See This Woman? A Liberative Look at Luke 7.36–50 and Strategies for Reading Other Lukan Stories against the Grain', in *A Feminist Companion to Luke*, ed. Amy-Jill Levine with Marianne Blickenstaff (Sheffield Academic Press, London, 2002), p. 113.

5 Klyne R. Snodgrass, *Stories with Intent: A Comprehensive Guide to the Parables of Jesus* (Eerdmans, Grand Rapids MI, 2008), p. 86.

6 *Stories with Intent*, p. 86.

7 Richard Bauckham, *Gospel Women: Studies of the Named Women in the Gospels* (T. & T. Clark, London and New York, 2002), p. 114.

8 Morna D. Hooker, *The Gospel According to Mark* (A. & C. Black, London, 1991), p. 328.

9 The love poetry of the Song of Songs is remarkable in the Bible for the woman's voice being as prominent as the man's, and it is her words that both open and close the collection of poems.

10 The translation is that of Robert Fagles, *Homer, The Odyssey* (Viking Penguin, New York, 2003), p. 405.

11 Ched Myers, *Binding the Strong Man: A Political Reading of Mark's Story of Jesus* (Orbis Books, Maryknoll NY, 1988), p. 359.

12 Elizabeth Schussler Fiorenza, *In Memory of Her: A Feminist Theological Reconstruction of Christian Origins*, 2nd edn (SCM Press, London, 1995), p. xliii.

13 John J. Pilch, *Healing in the New Testament: Insights from Medical and Mediterranean Anthropology* (Fortress Press, Minneapolis, 2000), p. 41.

14 *Binding the Strong Man*, p. 191.

15 *Binding the Strong Man*, p. 192.

16 Trevor Dennis, *Face to Face with God: Moses, Eluma and Job* (SPCK, London, 1999), p. 6.

17 James D. G. Dunn, *Christianity in the Making, Volume 1: Jesus Remembered* (Eerdmans, Grand Rapids MI, 2003), pp. 308–9; see also p. 674, n. 279.

18 D. E. Nineham, *The Gospel of St Mark* (Penguin, Harmondsworth, 1963), p. 151.

19 A phrase from William Vanstone's celebrated hymn, 'Morning glory, starlit sky'.

2 'The Vikings were all men'

1 Lucy Jolin, 'Rot Stopped,' *Cam*, Issue 74 (Lent 2015), p. 23.

2 For a convenient summary of the evidence, see Amy-Jill Levine in *The Jewish Annotated New Testament*, pp. 502–3.

3 John Dominic Crossan and Jonathan L. Reed, *Excavating Jesus: Beneath the Stories, Behind the Texts* (SPCK, London, 2001), p. 81. See also Jonathan L. Reed's discussion of the Gospels' description of Capernaum as 'a city' in *Archaeology and the Galilean Jesus* (Trinity Press International, Harrisburg PA, 2000), pp. 166–9.

4 Pierson Parker in *The Interpreter's Dictionary of the Bible*, vol. 1, ed. George Arthur Buttrick (Abingdon, Nashville, 1962), p. 845.

5 The NRSV has 'your mother and your brothers and sisters are outside', but many ancient manuscripts lack the addition 'and sisters', and *The Greek New Testament*, 3rd edn, puts the phrase in square brackets to indicate that it probably does not belong to the original text. There is no such doubt about the wording of the final verse in the passage, and it would seem some copyists were trying to make the earlier verse conform with that.

6 *In Memory of Her*, p. 147.

7 *The Gospel of St Mark*, p. 225.

8 So Morna Hooker in *The Gospel According to Mark*, p. 206.

9 See my comments in *The Easter Stories* (SPCK, London, 2008), pp. 58–61.

10 Joel B. Green, *The Gospel of Luke* (Eerdmans, Grand Rapids MI, 1997), p. 828.

11 Warren Carter, *Matthew and the Margins: A Socio-Political and Religious Reading* (Sheffield Academic Press, Sheffield, 2000), p. 358.

12 N. Clayton Croy, *The Mutilation of Mark's Gospel* (Abingdon Press, Nashville, 2003), p. 58.

13 N. T. Wright, *The Resurrection of the Son of God* (SPCK, London, 2003), pp. 617–24.

14 I discuss Mary's story in *The Easter Stories*, pp. 61–71.

15 Both sermons were in story form and can be found in my collection, *God in our Midst* (SPCK, London, 2012), pp. 84–9 and 89–93.

16 *Gospel Women*, pp. 109–202.

17 *Gospel Women*, pp. 135–8.

18 *Gospel Women*, p. 145; the quotation from Freyne is from Sean Freyne, *Galilee, Jesus and the Gospels* (Fortress, Philadelphia, 1988), p. 147.

19 *Gospel Women*, p. 149.

20 *Gospel Women*, p. 165.

21 *Gospel Women*, p. 196.

22 *Face to Face with God*, p. 20.

23 Loveday Alexander, 'Sisters in Adversity: Retelling Martha's Story', in *A Feminist Companion to Luke*, p. 198.

24 Warren Carter, 'Getting Martha out of the Kitchen: Luke 10.38–42 Again', in *A Feminist Companion to Luke*, p. 217.

25 'Sisters in Adversity', p. 213.

26 Diarmaid MacCulloch, *Silence: A Christian History* (Allen Lane, London, 2013), p. 34.

27 Raymond E. Brown, *The Gospel According to John XIII–XXI* (Doubleday, New York, 1970), p. 424.

28 *Healing in the New Testament*, p. 133.

29 Mona West, 'The Raising of Lazarus: A Lesbian Coming Out Story', in *A Feminist Companion to John*, vol. 1, ed. Amy-Jill Levine (Sheffield Academic Press, London, 2003), pp. 153, 154.

30 Mark W. G. Stibbe, *John* (Sheffield Academic Press, Sheffield, 1993), pp. 124, 125.

31 See Stibbe, *John*, p. 126.

32 See Raymond E. Brown, *The Gospel According to John I–XII* (Doubleday, New York, 1966), p. xcv. Brown discusses various theories of who the disciple might be on pp. xciii–xcviii.

33 See A. Brenner and F. van Dijk-Hemmes, *On Gendering Texts: Female and Male Voices in the Hebrew Bible* (E. J. Brill, Leiden, 1993).

34 *Gospel Women*, p. 14.

35 *Gospel Women*, p. 14.

3 Rejection rejected . . . and reinstated

1 Kenneth E. Bailey, *Poet and Peasant* (Eerdmans, Grand Rapids MI, 1980), p. 158.

2 *Stories with Intent*, p. 117.

3 Bernard Brandon Scott, *Hear Then the Parable: A Commentary on the Parables of Jesus* (Fortress Press, Minneapolis, 1989), p. 99.

4 James D. G. Dunn, 'Remembering Jesus: How the Quest of the Historical Jesus Lost its Way', in *The Historical Jesus: Five Views*, ed. James K. Beilby and Paul R. Eddy (SPCK, London, 2010), p. 215.

5 'Remembering Jesus' in *The Historical Jesus: Five Views*, p. 215.

6 I discuss the story at some length, and the ways in which so many interpretations have distorted it, in *Sarah Laughed: Women's Voices in the Old Testament* (SPCK, London, 1994), pp. 8–33.

7 Amy-Jill Levine, *Short Stories by Jesus: The Enigmatic Parables of a Controversial Rabbi* (HarperCollins, New York, 2014), p.18.

8 *Short Stories by Jesus*, pp. 36–7.

9 Nicodemus' lack of comprehension mirrors the failure of other male disciples to understand Jesus. His wavering in John 3 is to be contrasted with the enthusiasm of the Samaritan woman in John 4, who runs back to her village and cries, 'Come and see a man who told me everything I have ever done! He cannot be the Messiah, can he?' (4.29). Here we have another case, which unfortunately we did not have space to explore in the last chapter, of a woman who gets it and a man who, for the moment, does not.

10 Chapter 1 of Levine's book *Short Stories by Jesus* is entitled, 'Lost Sheep, Lost Coin, Lost Son'. We should add that this does not in any way cramp her style when she reaches the third parable.

11 *Short Stories by Jesus*, p. 39.

12 Kenneth E. Bailey, *Jacob and the Prodigal: How Jesus Retold Israel's Story* (BRF, Oxford, 2003).

13 *Stories with Intent*, p. 130.

14 Jonathan Sacks, *Not in God's Name: Confronting Religious Violence* (Hodder and Stoughton, London, 2015), pp. 102–3.

15 Joseph A. Fitmyer, *The Gospel According to Luke X–XXIV* (Doubleday, New York, 1985), p. 1082.

16 *Stories with Intent*, p. 131.

17 *Short Stories by Jesus*, p. 56.

18 See *Short Stories by Jesus*, p. 56.

19 Trevor Dennis, *Lo and Behold! The Power of Old Testament Storytelling* (SPCK, London, 1991), pp. 45–6. The scene where Laban puts poor Leah in Jacob's bed is found in Genesis 29.15–25.

20 *Lo and Behold!*, p. 48.

21 See *Lo and Behold!*, p. 57 and my discussion of the use of the Hebrew term *berakhah* in Genesis 33.11.

22 *Short Stories by Jesus*, pp. 63–4.

23 The NRSV translates 'a long robe with sleeves'. The Hebrew phrase, *ketonet pasim*, appears in only one other passage, 2 Samuel 13.18, where it describes the apparel of a princess. Robert Alter, who himself translates 'an ornamented tunic', provides a useful note in *The Five Books of Moses: A Translation with Commentary* (W. W. Norton, New York, 2004), p. 207.

24 As is the case with the shepherd and the woman in The Lost Sheep and The Lost Coin.

25 That is my own translation. It might seem too free, but it captures, so I believe, the spirit of the Hebrew and the anger being expressed. 'Why the hell?' is an especially bold rendering, but there is a little word in the Hebrew which most translators ignore that gives the language a force a simple 'why?' does not convey.

26 *Face to Face with God*, p. 19.

27 The elder son speaks of his father denying him 'a young goat' to eat with his friends. That particular detail might recall Rebekah saying to Jacob in Genesis 27.9, 'Go to the flock and get me two choice kids, so that I may prepare from them savoury food for your father, such as he likes.' However, the echoes of Jacob's speech to Laban are more numerous and far more significant.

28 *Hear Then the Parable*, p. 108.

29 Scott agrees: see *Hear Then the Parable*, p. 122.

30 *Not in God's Name*, p. 115.

31 I sum up my assessment of Sarah, as she is portrayed in Genesis, in that very phrase in *Sarah Laughed*, p. 61.

32 See *Sarah Laughed*, pp. 67–73.

33 *Not in God's Name*, p. 115.

34 Sacks discusses the ambiguities presented by the Hebrew of this verse in *Not in God's Name*, pp. 139–40.

35 Psalm 137.7 conveys a similar fury and bitterness against the Edomites.

36 *Not in God's Name*, p. 169.

37 *Not in God's Name*, pp. 95–6.

38 *Not in God's Name*, p. 97.

39 See, for example, Numbers 11.11–15. I explore this remarkable passage in *Face to Face with God*, pp. 21–5, and we will discuss it briefly in the next chapter of this book.

40 In each of those two Gospels these are the only words Jesus speaks from the cross.

4 'Here is God: no monarch he, throned in easy state to reign'

1 See Levine and Brettler in *The Jewish Annotated New Testament*, p. 34 (the note on Matthew 18.21–22).

2 Everett Fox's translation of a phrase in Genesis 1.31 which is more usually rendered as 'very good': *The Five Books of Moses* (Harvill Press, London, 1995), p. 17.

3 The words quoted are taken from an article by Jonathan Jones in *The Guardian* of 7 January 2016 on an exhibition of women's art: 'Raise your glasses to 14 women and 14 chances to correct the history of art'.

4 *Matthew and the Margins*, pp. 372–3.

5 *Matthew and the Margins*, p. 374.

6 The phrase is taken from the title of a famous book by Phyllis Trible, *Texts of Terror: Literary–Feminist Readings of Biblical Narratives* (Fortress Press, Philadelphia, 1984).

7 *Christianity in the Making, Volume 1: Jesus Remembered*, p. 425.

8 *Jesus Remembered*, p. 422, n. 211.

9 *Stories with Intent* , p. 27.

10 *Stories with Intent*, p. 31.

11 John Dominic Crossan, 'Response to Robert M. Price', in *The Historical Jesus: Five Views*, p. 87.

12 John Dominic Crossan, *Jesus and the Violence of Scripture: How to Read the Bible and Still be a Christian* (SPCK, London, 2015), pp. 176–8.

13 *Jesus and the Violence of Scripture*, p. 163.

14 See Walter Brueggemann, *Theology of the Old Testament: Testimony, Dispute, Advocacy* (Fortress Press, Minneapolis, 1997), pp. 234–61.

15 *Theology of the Old Testament*, p. 238.

16 In Exodus 15.1 the song is ascribed to Moses, but other passages in the Old Testament suggest it was women who composed such victory songs. The whole of it, not just the one verse in Exodus 15.21, should be called the Song of Miriam.

17 Marvin E. Tate, *Word Biblical Commentary: Psalms 51–100* (Word Books, Dallas, 1990), p. 240.

18 My own translation. Though it differs from the commonly used versions, including the NRSV, it follows the lead of a number of Job scholars: see *Face to Face with God*, pp. 108–9 and p. 117, n. 31.

19 Helen Schungel-Straumann, 'God as Mother in Hosea 11', in *A Feminist Companion to the Latter Prophets*, ed. Athalya Brenner (Sheffield Academic Press, Sheffield, 1995), p. 196 (for the translation), pp. 200–202 (for the discussion of it).

20 For other Old Testament passages where the image of God as mother appears, see: Deuteronomy 32.18; Isaiah 42.14, 45.10, 46.3–4, 66.13.

21 See Craig A. Evans, *Jesus and his World: The Archaeological Evidence* (SPCK, London, 2012), pp. 13–14.

22 See Brown, *The Gospel According to John I–XII*, p. 330.

23 Trevor Dennis, *The Christmas Stories* (SPCK, London, 2007), p. 48.

24 For the thinking behind this reconstruction see *The Christmas Stories*, pp. 107–9.

25 'Messiah' is a Hebrew word, meaning 'anointed' or 'anointed one'; 'Christos' is its Greek equivalent.

26 The opening line is from Isaiah 62.11, the rest from Zechariah 9.9.

27 See *Jesus and the Violence of Scripture*, pp. 29–30.

28 Marcus Borg and John Dominic Crossan, *The Last Week: What the Gospels Really Teach about Jesus' Final Days in Jerusalem* (SPCK, London, 2008), p. 3.

29 *The Last Week*, p. 2.

30 Other examples in the Old Testament of prophets acting out their prophecies can be found in Jeremiah 13.1–7 (not that Jeremiah could have performed such an act to the letter); Ezekiel 12.1–7, 21.6, 18–20, 24.15–24 (a most poignant passage, concerning the death of the prophet's wife), 37.15–23. See also Acts 21.10–11, where a Christian prophet

named Agabus takes Paul's belt and with it binds his own hands and feet, to demonstrate the fate awaiting Paul in Jerusalem.

31 See my discussion in *The Easter Stories*, pp. 88–90.

32 *Not in God's Name*, p. 222 (the italics are his).

33 *Not in God's Name*, p. 225 (the italics are his).

Flo's Story

A little story about prayer

After I was widowed, my daughter Jo persuaded me to go to this tea dance in a church hall, a bus ride away from where I live. It was a way to keep fit and meet a few people and really cheered me up, but I still felt empty inside.

One day Dot, the lady who runs the dances, was handing out these little *Prayers on the Move* booklets, so I took one. I hadn't been to church for years and I hadn't prayed for a long time, but reading this little book, by myself, in my own time, the prayers really spoke to me. I realized what had been missing.

The next week, I told Dot that I'd really enjoyed the book and said I thought it would be nice to go to church. Dot said she'd give me a lift. Now I'm going to church every Sunday, I've found my faith again and I'm so happy. That empty feeling inside has gone away and it's all thanks to a little booklet called *Prayers on the Move*.

Inspired by a true story. Names and places have been changed.

Help us to tell more stories like Flo's. Sign up for the newsletter, buy bags, books and travelcard wallets, and make a donation to help more people like Flo find God through a book. www.prayersonthemove.com.